Murmuration Archives

Felicia Zamora

Published by Noemi Press, Inc. A Nonprofit Literary organization. www.noemipress.org.

Cover & Book Design by Roda Avelar
Typeset in Edita Book and Spinoza Pro

ISBN: 978-1-955992-71-8

Murmuration Archives

Felicia Zamora

Archives/Murmurs

Flocking :: Leaking

Visual Invitation to Attract

Dilution Effect

More Eyes Toward Detection

Now it still ripples, now it still murmurs, ripples, it still sighs, still hums, and it is empty under sky.

Unknown, *Popol Vuh*

Inceptions

The Codex Yoalli Ehēcatl is one of the few ancient Mesoamerican sacred texts to survive the Spanish colonization of Mexico. The document is also known by its colonized name, Codex Borgia. Under 20 codices from the pre-Columbian Mesoamerican era exist today. The Mesoamerican codices fall into three groups: Mixtecan histories, Maya religious books and highland religious books, and the Borgia Group with the Codex Yoalli Ehēcatl (Codex Borgia) being the most prominent member. The Borgia Group holds specific significance due to the pre-conquest date and the religious content held within.

The Codex Yoalli Ehēcatl is a ritual book for prognostication and divination—depictions of a long supernatural journey, patterns for ceremonies on the installation of rulers, a catalogue of supernatural beings who influence the world, and more. Calendrical in places, the Codex contains an almanac involving the Tōnalpōhualli, a version of the 260-day solar calendar which consists of 20 trecenas (13-day) periods. Tōnalpōhualli in Nahuatl means "counting of days." The 20-day signs (Reed, Rabbit, Water, Jaguar, Movement (also known as Ollin), Flint, and others) and the five directions (the four cardinal and the Center being the hinge that constitutes the fifth of space, time, and the supernatural world) are all visible within the Codex. The cast of deities in the Codex range from more iconic gods such as Quetzalcōātl and the Nine Lords of the Night, to deities that inhabit multiple names, faces, purposes, and powers, to deities that are unknown.

Much of the Codex remains shrouded in mystery. The exact location of creation, the authors, how many authors, intent of the document, what language the authors spoke, and what language was used in the syllabary and hieroglyphs are all unknown. Some scholars believe the Codex originated in the 1400s around the Southern Puebla or Northeastern Oaxaca regions.

The Codex Yoalli Ehēcatl now lives in the Vatican Apostolic Library in Vatican City. The high-resolution images of the Codex are held in the Ancient Americas exhibit at the Los Angeles County Museum of Art (LACMA).

Undulations

These poems contain fragments of encounters with the Codex Yoalli Ehēcatl in the Vatican Apostolic Library, visiting Chichén Itzá, and being diagnosed with breast cancer all within a four-month span. Vibrations felt. I am shaped from ancestors, shaped from those who dwelled on Earth before me, shaped from what dwells inside me. I am sculpting and sculpture. I form from pressures of time, colonization, gaps in lineage, cells, experiences, conditionings, disease, beloveds, and instincts. In the searching, in wonderment, in inextricable longing, these communions with the Codex Yoalli Ehēcatl emerged.

Flocking :: Leaking

These places will leak their histories and will void; they will burn lines into the walls of the page and will haunt the periphery with figuration.

Renee Gladman, *Plans for Sentences*

Undulation (n.) (v.)

un·du·la·tion (ən-je-ˈlā-SHən)

1. : moving, smooth rise, smooth fall of form, of outline
2. : wave-esque motion, in elastic or fluid medium; continuous particle propagation; non-permanence of particle translation
    1. : motion of collective particles & non-permanence (See: "A movement comes into existence to transform what is in existence." — Sara Ahmed, *Living a Feminist Life*)
3. : vibration; pulsation from two tones seeking; longing of unison (See also: Throat Full of Absent Spanish) (See also: Throat Full of Absent Nahuatl)
4. : Vicuña knows; urges, a guide (See: *Instan*)
5. : *the gentle undulation of your body holding the Codex Yoalli Ehēcatl* (See also: Interior Energy)
6. : Ollin, or movement; ancient symbol in the Codex Yoalli Ehēcatl; one of the 260 calendrical day signs of the Tōnalpōhualli (See: ancient hieroglyph below)
    1. what makes you cross an ocean; what the Vatican keeps; what cracks your neck in prayer for you chanting *arrive arrive arrive arrive*; what makes you pulsate indefinitely
7. : preverbal/more-than-verbal/unable-verbal response to the Codex Yoalli Ehēcatl (See also: Bodily Awe) (See also: Blood Lineage Awakening) (See also: Once Asleep, Now Wake) (See also: Ecstatic Marrow)

{Quetzalcōātl, God of Life, Back To}

Think dual, not duel. From amniotic
lung: extrapolation: a promise: what grows
will grow. Know what you carry
with you—on your back, in veins, in
larynx, in your cardiac muscle, in keratin
of your nail plate. Hair & toenails
considered *skin appendages*. Weight of all
that appendages you. How the God
of Wind & God of Life inhabit the same
body—in a belief where one deity
metamorphosizes to another
& another. You lust the uncertainty
of morphology. You practice
linguistics as prayer & still what fastens
to you reminds, *I am always here*. How you
breathe & the act is godliness. The air,
god. A version of you always facing outward
stave poised for ceremony, for fight.

{26 Consecutive Days/20 Day Signs ::
A Lament On Missing}

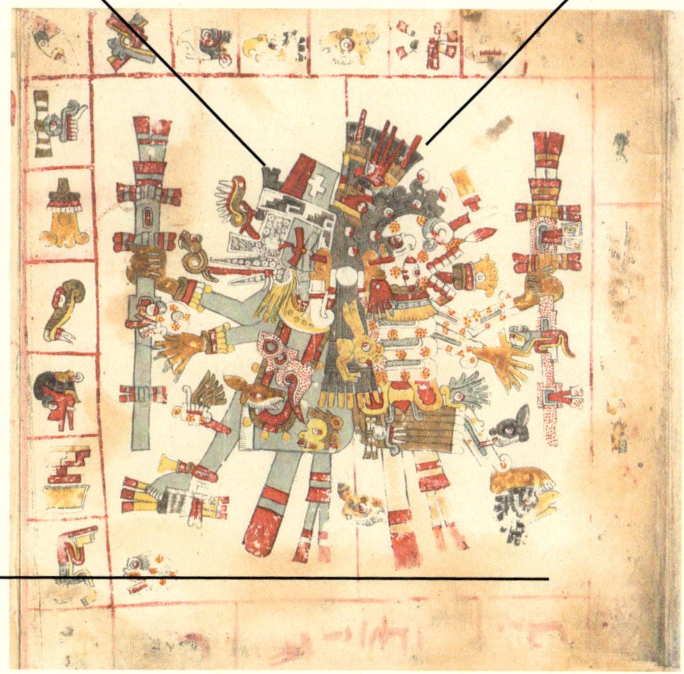

{Mictlāntēcutli, God of
Death, Back To}

Flower tongue—to unfurl
in a field of tree dahlias
between the jaws of a god. Aztec
word, *acocotil*, water-cane,
hollow stems once used
to transport water. Hollowness
haunts you now. You who obsess
with origins. All that originates
in the mountains of Mexico. Where
return nestles behind your molars
year over year, until you strip
of organs & strip of need to use
those organs & the only judgement
not falsified is *when*. You stand
before the God of the Underworld,
drink from a watery knee, feel
the soft phantasm lick across
petals of your cheeks, pet the dog
nestled at shin, saying, *I know you.*

When you begin at an end, you catch smoke in your lungs rather than smoke through your fingers. How a heparinized saline solution in a Port-A-Cath maintains patency & tastes of Band-Aids in the throat. Band-Aid without the Band-Aid. Because you know this means an end & beginning occurred. Ten years ago, a gesture formed in lobules of your breast; a whisper not wanted or ancient yet broken out of glands. Some stories you count days. Some stories you count centuries. You pray to Patency, God of Unobstruction of Flesh. The missing means *once here*. Ends & beginnings are nothing more than demarcations; a falseness that echoes & echoes & echoes &

Xibalbá :: Tunneling

Division. How we splice & splice & splice, mentally & anatomically. A cell becomes cells becomes exponential cells. A gorging. Always, our becoming; our something tangled in multiplicity. How the body yearns to rewild from behind muscle & bone. Singh's "an infinite collection of bodyings" consumes me. I stand at the mirror each morning to introduce my face to my idea of my face.

*

Outside the Walgreens' parking lot, the nurse's voice translated me. *The tumor is malignant.*

*

In Maya tradition, the universe split into three realms: celestial vault, Earth, & Xibalbá. Western hierarchical thinking of *do good to avoid a torturous after-life* or *bad deeds = various forms of hell*, were not part of the ancient Maya belief system. To avoid Xibalbá, you sought a violent death. Does death exist beyond a violent one? The severing of one realm into another. I might be wrong. Wrong to believe the tunneling, the emergence *from* liquid, our life *as* liquid, *back through* liquid must mean something. I often confuse *meaning* with *chaos*.

*

The tympanic membrane made of sheer tissue vibrates with each sound wave—a type of memorying that splits & splits. Where I am in the bodying process? In speaking here, I split a little more.

*

I read the arguments on all births being violent. I disagree. In our pluralist inhabitations, we were never meant to stay wombed. Our once-small bodies designed to pass through, to canal, canal, canal, our way from anaerobic breath to aerobic breath. Outside our mother, we begin deterioration; grow & deteriorate, grow & deteriorate. An inescapable order.

*

A cell becomes cells becomes exponential cells. & cancer infiltrates some of those cells. Some cells deadly. & death becomes a bullet point on a list.

*

Habitual. I crack my knuckles & visualize cancerous lymph nodes. Habitual. I chew my cuticle & see the empty space where breast tissue once lived. Habitual. I bite my lower lip & the surgery scheduler asks, *Did you fill out the Ohio power of attorney document? Who will make your decisions if you cannot be resuscitated?* In constant shed, in passing tunnel after tunnel, rewilding occurs.

*

I count bullet points, make lists inside lists. Xibalbá, how much violence is enough violence?

In question, I split, then split the split.

Upon Remembering the Statistic[i]

You scan the city from the top of Palatine Hill
while the others from your tour group melt
into clusters of figures. Hazy scatters from a hazy
mind thousands of miles west. West of?[ii] You
interrogate your own definitions. Even the wind
melts you a little. What you bring here: two
wonders: one, the length of time a body
carries any hungry thing in its cellular pouches;
two, the number of times you say *my body my body*
my body before this unencompassing word
drains from you, pools into a conjured inky
blot that walks beside you, brushes your hair
from your forehead, holds your hand, takes
your shoulders, turns you to look at all shadows
& outlines saying, *What grows inside you*
entered uninvited. & you shake.[iii] Your beloved
slides arms around your waist & you change
subject to the heat, wobbly earbuds, the long-winded
tour guide. You think about horizons.[iv] How history

turns on sharp edges. Who gets sliced in the turn?[v]

You believe in chaos theory, yet ask *Where do the prayers*

of my atheist heart go?[vi] You mention the Colosseum's

brutality. For the rest of the tour, you roll *brutal, brutal,*

brutal, brutal, brutal, brutal in the back of your throat.

---

[i] On average breast cancer develops over 8-10 years in the body before discovered. This in your breast cancer handbook the surgeon gave you.

[ii] You waffle between the use/nonuse of *home* in this moment. So you do not use it. You choose to use it here. The body as home, how we carry it with us. What if home becomes compromised?

[iii] You ask yourself who/what is real. This is the wrong question. When does anything first become real? Gloria Anzaldúa reminds us that the real begins in the images in our minds first.

[iv] Two weeks from now, your mastectomy surgery scheduled. This is where the poem becomes accurate/inaccurate in the necessary ways of consumption of the real. What exists/does not exist outside this poetic world?

[v] The surgeon told you thirty lymph nodes may be removed in an axillary dissection. You obsess with nuclei. Someone once called Palatine Hill the "first nucleus of the Roman empire." Body of evolving empires.

[vi] You doubt your allowance to pray. As if praying were attached to the *entity* of prayer versus the *act of*. All the acts you doubt now. When is an act enough?

You are pretending. You are pretending. You are pretending. You are pre
You are pretending. You are pretending. You are pretending. You are pre
You are pretending. You are pretending. You are pretending. You are pre
You are pretending. You are pretending. You are pretending. You are pre
You are pretending. You are pretending. You are pretending. You are pre
You are pretending. You are pretending. You are pretending. You are pre
You are pretending. You are pretending. You are pretending. You are pre
You are pretending. You are pretending. You are pretending. You are pre

tending. You are pretending. You are pretending. You are
tending. You are pretending. You are pretending. You are
tending. You are pretending. You are pretending. You are
tending. You are pretending. You are pretending. You are
tending. You are pretending. You are pretending. You are
tending. You are pretending. You are pretending. You are
tending. You are pretending. You are pretending. You are
tending. You are pretending. You are pretending. You are

pretending. You are pretending. You are pretending you.
pretending. You are pretending. You are pretending you.
pretending. You are pretending. You are pretending you.
pretending. You are pretending. You are pretending you.
pretending. You are pretending. You are pretending you.
pretending. You are pretending. You are pretending you.
pretending. You are pretending. You are pretending you.
pretending. You are pretending. You are pretending you.

You are pretending. You are pretending. You are pretending.
You are pretending. You are pretending. You are pretending.
You are pretending. You are pretending. You are pretending.
You are pretending. You are pretending. You are pretending.
You are pretending. You are pretending. You are pretending.
You are pretending. You are pretending. You are pretending.
You are pretending. You are pretending. You are pretending.
You are pretending. You are pretending. You are pretending.

September 14, 2022, Palatine Hill, Rome. 14 days before mastectomy.

Archive Notes #1 :: Codex Yoalli Ehēcatl, Vatican Apostolic Library, September 2022

flip
casing
preserve

plates raw evidence of water damage
plates collapsed
burnt before Borgia

Severe damage on pages
Penciled numbers burn
marks tactic for

missing
faded
reconstruction

journey of the viewer
seeks understanding

Feet feet feet
feet on Wind, Dog, Deer, Flower
blank, see the textures
veins damage in
"MESSICANO I"
placed in front of me
read I
felt wild
weight of a thing weight of
lineage ancestry codex space

path

changed
seam

creates
seam

exquisite

image

transports

in a stiff

ink remains

larger than seen

I Carry a Wor{l}d Inside Me

Where wor{l}d & the tangible object of that wor{l}d collide. Traces. & again, Singh's words at the back of my throat, "The unconscious is the most evasive archive of all, yet is pulsing right there inside you." How the brain talks through & within epithelial barriers. Porous borders. How the brain chatters. Yet in the world of synapses, even the brain may not know-know. Language an archive. Flesh an archive. Felt presence. When what you feel supersedes the imaging. *The mammogram cleared.* & so. & so. What we keep hungry in the dark. What keeps. How much depends on a cell. Cell. I carry a wor{l}d inside me. What wraps tightly amongst the organs. Cells that do not mature, forgo the process of differentiation to reproduce, reproduce, reproduce. A silent stalking. I carry a wor{l}d inside me. A wor{l}d unimpressed with naming, with its own name. & this name; this name. I speak this wor{l}d so often, my tongue tastes of dandelion sap. Let me say *tissues.* Four types of tissues reside in the human body: connective, epithelial, muscle, & nervous. Connective tissues bind & support by holding together blood, bone & lymphatic tissues. How the epithelial covers— the skin & the linings of various passages become noticeable, heightened. Tender {e}motions, veins, muscles of me. To deconstruct. Inside the wor{l}d lives other wor{l}ds. Clever brain, always making games. To deconstruct *tissues: tis-tis, uses, us, sits, is, sues, issues.* Ah, there, *issues. Issues. Issues.* Deeper still: *revolt, sickening, gorge-gorge, invasive.* Deeper still: *relinquish, nipple-tugged-down, ten-centimeter incision, harvest, ghost of a breast, neuropathy, echoing empty lymph nodes space, carcinoma.* Deeper still, until gutturals, until no archive left to h{a}unt.

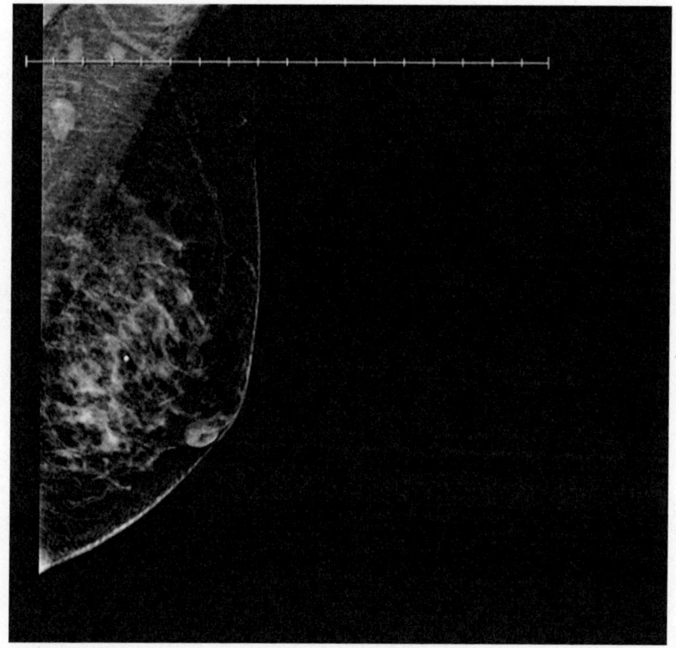

Xibalbá :: How One Body Carries

You stand outside the Group of a Thousand Columns in the rain. Tropical rain. Your Ohio drizzle feels shameful. You feel rain on your nipples. Temptation. Later, *nipples* become singular. *No, not yet. You lack foreshadowing*. You falseness. Foreshadow. You lack concentration. *I traveled all this way. Shit, even the Dramamine kicked in*. You try to hold your camera up in the water-tight bag. Fuzzy blots on the lens. *How am I supposed to document*? You scold your tourist thoughts. *My heart wants to be in this*. How do you know what your heart thinks? You think of the website. What these columns symbolize: internal consciousness of a human comprised of psychological defect after psychological defect after defect after defect into the tens of thousands of thousands of defects. How one body carries all these defects. We also carry facets of warriors. All the warrior traits fighting the defects inside. Somewhere you read "evil inside." You sigh *& if what's inside is me*? You don't believe in binaries. Your saints wrap in sinners & vice versa. You put your phone away in a drenched pocket & stand with the pillars. Each droplet a baptism. Each hair on your body rises to attention.

New Ritual: Codex Yoalli Ehēcatl Visit, Vatican Apostolic Library, September 2022

I went to hold you with pupils & inadequate tongue. Then hands—my hands without gloves on your ancient body. Animal skin body surviving. Pre-Columbian pre-conquest of Mexico. Gaps in dates, 1200 to 1500 AD. All unknowns of artists of language of region. Uncertainty: an accordion of once-worn flesh removed from beast & painted in images of gods. Divination in blood. 260-day ritual calendar of ceremony of journeys of sacrifice & transformation. My fingers run the same grooves, same hieroglyphs drawn by my ancestors. *Home*: a word I absorb in water-damaged, fire -damaged pages. Here among scholars— required quiet of archives & Swiss Guard— I am the beast. Beast within walls of god— unbeliever, unrighteous, unfaithful to singular ideas of creator— knowing chaos creates her own untethering to culture to language to sharpness of colonization's history. Subjugation masquerades as integration & my mother's shame became my wound & my wound became resistance to my own ownness. Sin lengua in Spanish. Unpious in English. Unknowing of fists in my chest when they place in front of me. Wrapped in wood, laid bare. To read you left to right—*as if I could read you at all*—I must turn you, babe-like, upside down. Turn you to see your gifts given right to left. Turn you again babe-like on your axis to follow your journey. A vertical, snaking journey. I stand. Then squat next to you. I stand. Then squat next to you. My knees & elbows bow. I embrace a new ritual: *I am yours*.

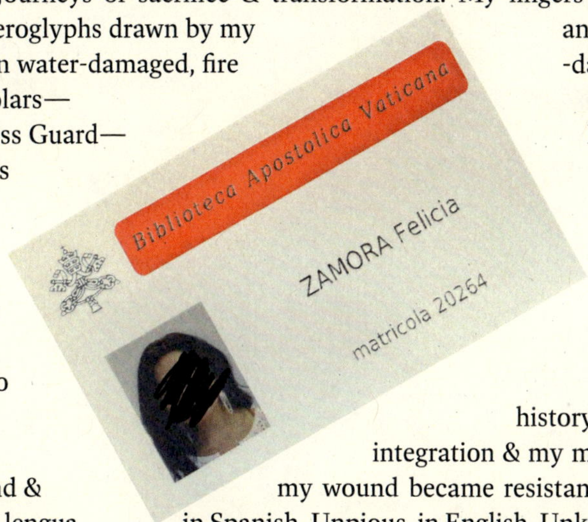

17 Days After Mastectomy & Axillary Dissection of Lymph Nodes: A Love Poem

We think we let the world in—
how oxidation slowly turns the avocado
dimple by lovely dimple
from green to brown to black; oxygen
how we react to polyphenols, how
enzymes love us too much, too wanting
wringing with desire, slick & wet & biochemical
so we must breathe in the soot & we must
exhale our own toxins; *the way of any living*
thing is to live, they say; what if all the *theys*
are wrong? what if the living never came
easy in the first place? what if I keep
removing pieces of me: shuck of appendix,
shuck of gallbladder, shuck of knee, now,
shuck of breast, shuck of nodes? cenotes
of us: carved from our tissues, our fluid-filled ____;
where we must & always swim—but we were wrong.
We world, wholly; planet of flesh, ripening.
Let wind, let sun consume; fruit of us
to elements; let's engulf & gulp in remembering
w/holes: the whole world claws & thunders inside
these vessels, this lymphatic system to make us
immune—*as if, as if*—immune to what? Parts of us
let go into stars beyond this planet: call these *petri-*
dish bound, call these *cancer evictions*; what I know
of never returning: a star before supernova senses
the future rupture: premonition echoes: *transform.*

{Obscure Moon with a Rabbit Inside}

Sun reflects the moon's surfaces. Divinate this. Outside the Alden Motel, asparagus grew wild. Divinate this. Before this. Before you ate asparagus. Before you knew of sulfurous biproducts in asparagusic acid. Before your partner whose genetic make-up makes him & his family unable to smell the asparagus odor from urine. Divinate this. Before you Google *Best Ways to Prepare Asparagus*. Only six when Grandma Evelyn scours the ditch picking stalks near the rusted barbed wire. Tells you, *This makes good* ___ . All the good making; emptiness of what comes after *good*; memories smudge. You left to divinate gaps. When moon arrives, crickets fill thick heat & dewy corn across the old Highway 20. Asparagus peeking; all moonlight bathes—dances of what arrives to nibble & pick under canopies of dark. You, too, born wild, in an obscure cradle hung haphazardly celestial in someone else's sky.

{One Butterfly}

Among the plumes. Among twelve birds. Mistaken for bird—amoeba wings. Solar deity, Tōnatiuh centers you; how often godliness seeks *ownness* in image. Look at you, full of flutter, counting dot after dot after dot. Time's continuous representation. In particularities, any flying creature, any winged companion; again with representation. You among thirteen levels of creation, curve in shape of a magnet; all that pulls you above the plane of Earth.

{Jaws of the Earth Monster with Quail's Head}

Are you not cranium catalytic, delicately placed in the jaws/laws of soil? Munch of any bone. A peachness to your skull. Tinder of tender. Any bone munches. Lick of saliva. Often, you the quail head. Often, the monster.

Xibalbá :: Baby Teeth

The researcher finds children's bones, *Sacrifices in the cenotes*. Mayas recreated a stone road to Xibalbá in a cenote cave. *Fully intact*, the researcher's voice fluctuates. You lean into your screen. Take a lick of raspberry popsicle. You shiver a little. Not at the Xibalbá road. Shiver from eating a raspberry popsicle in January while watching documentaries about ancient Maya civilizations. The two are not mutually exclusive. Popsicles to soothe your mouth sores from the first two months of chemo. On the popsicle stick, a joke: *HOW DOES THE OCEAN GREET THE BEACH*? You lick on: *IT WAVES*. The all-capital letters. Yelling. Yelling over the machine that prints the jokes. Your mother on assembly line at Berry Plastics. Yogurt cup in hand as the foreman's yells bleed into gear hums. The foreman's chin opening. The joke-designers' chins; their mouths moving, in slow motion, as they shout: *WHAT KIND OF HORSE LIKES TO BE RIDDEN AT NIGHT*? You lick. *WHAT DO YOU CALL A HAPPY RABBIT*? Lick. Shiver. Lick. *WHY COULND'T THE BAKER BUY A NEW CAR*? Lick. Lick. Lick. *WHAT DO YOU CALL A SLEEPING COW*? Lick. Lick. Shiver. Lick. Lick. Do the joke designers think of their mandibles? What soothes versus stings. Or do the joke designers think of children's mandibles? Mandibles that will suck the popsicles & read the designers' jokes & think *That ain't funny*. Or will children's mandibles open wide, heads flung back to expose baby teeth. Baby teeth with porcelain crowns. Porcelain crowns cause their parents opted to listen to the orthodontist's warnings, *Protect the baby teeth now, so the permanent teeth don't rot*. All that children's mandibles & maxillae masticate. How a scream & a laugh may register similar in an echoing body of cave. How a scream & a laugh may register similar in a factory of echoing machines. How a scream & a laugh may register similar on a bathroom floor after infusion. All gapes & echoes. Children's mandibles open wide—cenote wide; wide as the top of the subterrane torn off; wide to reveal the roof of Xibalbá, sparkling in winks, where sun's rays illuminate down stone over bone until—the silence of enamel after enamel glistening in light.

Message to Rabbit in the Moon

Ixchel, I feel you crossing. Night womb. Tell me where the seeds go. One seedless keeper to seed-full keeper. A lunar field of sunflowers sprouts from my chest. Both of us caught, in cycles not our own.

Ecogodliness

I pause at the underbelly of a lily pad. The veins. My god the veins. I put my phone down & think of all the lily pads I've encountered, never once thinking of the underside. All I turn over, choose not to turn over. All ahead of me left to turn & turn. Who looms large from above, unknowing—or unwilling—to turn me from back to belly, to inspect my Achilles, then soles of my feet? Check my palms for residue? Pick at the etches in my wrists? Scan each follicle for what hides in passages between hair & epidermis? What lingers in the overlooked. *Linger with me*. Tracing veins & belly buttons. Our thick fingers on our not-so-smallness. Berssenbrugge said, "When we enter into that closeness and unboundedness, it feels like disintegration, like everywhere." *Gasp*—I acknowledge the vastness tucked inside *everywhere*. *Everywhere*: brain to galaxy, brain as galaxy. *Gasp*—mouth, too, a type of galaxy; language another. Energy collecting & expelling: propels the tumble & also the ghost in haunt of the tumble. Vastness in vastness. Think of a cell. Now the 100 trillion inside you. *Gasp*. Energy in a cell. What recycles. What churns. What burns away. Who disintegrates me. Who I disintegrate. What turns from me, unable to stomach my filthy veins. My filthy veins. Filthy filth. How I long despite. To show you my crevasses. *That* closeness. Closeness: a brandished, bleeding love story. *Don't forget to peer so close you taste the supernova on my breath*. What protrudes me. Am I lily pad? Am I frog? Am I hand turning? Or am I the water, forgotten, in hold of everything together?

Science of Undoing

You are an extreme   *reaction.* This is code

for: *I don't believe you.*   My body—

always a topic of doubt. In Mt. Airy Forest my sneakers

on concrete   pummel out   words   [*You shouldn't*

be in this much ________. (Her hand pushes   on swollen flesh.) *See this, this*

it's your back fat.   (I wince. I ache.)]

& the burn of 11 lymph nodes   not gone

missing, torn out   [How sometimes we must open

to the pain   to rid   to exterminate.]

in some Petri dish, some lab   before discard,

what we must discard,   as in all the cells

malignant—

as in all the words   that shudder & hunt   all the gorgeous cells   all

collection & sporing   all suckle suckle & latch   all colonizing—

[How many times must a body ________ & ideas of *endure* of *resilience* of *persistence*
glower in their lack.]

writing around a cell my cell/our cell [all wanting]. Etymology

of *take*.

What we ask the body to give up. What we ask the body to take. Who

takes? Who taken from? [*Call this economics*

of the body. No. Fuck no. My body holds enough science of undoing.]

Any wounded animal backed into a corner: lash, snarl, snarl, lash. [Do we ask

the tiger, *please explain* *the hurt?* We do this all wrong. Think

species here. Who gets to be *human*. Who labels *animal*. Who labels.]

In the exam room, why must I always be [lash, snarl, snarl, lash]

the animal. Without my consent,

words become another suckling, another latching cell.

Xibalbá :: Patience

Something waits. A protrusion. Muscles around a collarbone gather.

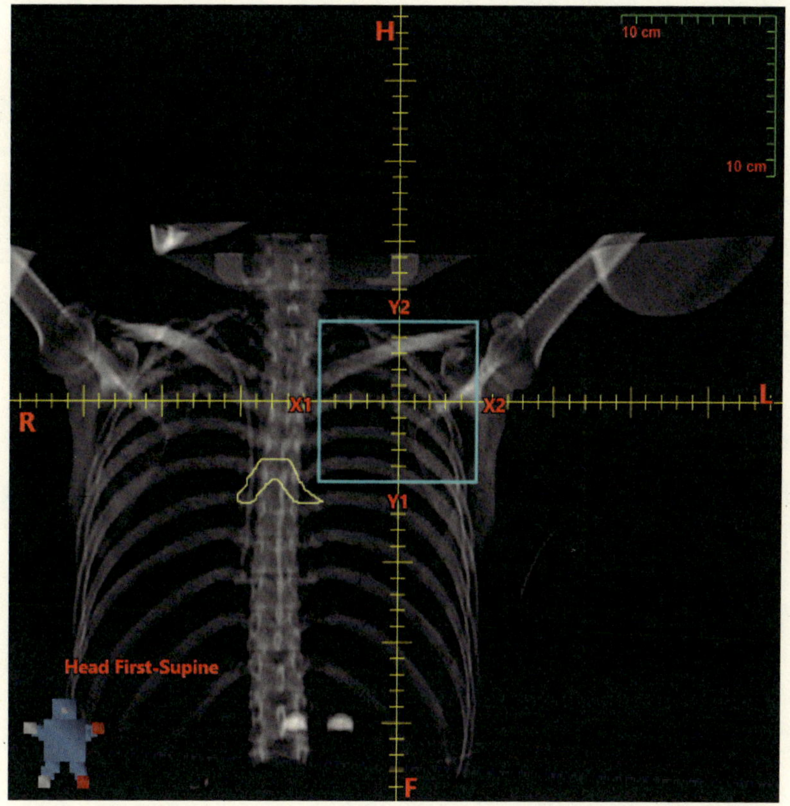

Archive Notes #2 :: Codex Yoalli Ehēcatl, Vatican Apostolic Library, September 2022

body
read incorrectly.
HOLE when you look through
place
of damage

hole middle middle
bandages

around the perimeter
Empty
weight of
hole
this symbol
Seam damage
seam
study more seam
fastened Seam
Study more
supernatural more
seam left
curious
rabbit in box
continues arrangement (seam robust seam)
contrast language vs.
syllabary Study this
convexing
seam
circles inside circles

figures gone
wiped away

fire around
binding
Weight is without

Xibalbá :: Offerings

An archaeologist found a cenote the size of six swimming pools below El Castillo. *Castle*, you smile thinking of Joe & the chess move he taught you at fourteen. In Scotland Joe confessed, *I want to live in a castle*. All rooks & moats as you tilt your wet head observing the stone balustrades. Puddles swell around the Temple of Kukulcán.

No surprise a cenote exists here, it's the pyramid built on top of it that's extraordinary, the archaeologist said. No one can reach the cenote without digging.

*

The Temple of Kukulcán built over a smaller temple. Did the builders know? What's inner-inner gnaws at you. Your almost-born body in your mother's womb. Were you the smaller temple destined to be inside her? All the empty temples inside you now.

How the ancient Maya reused structures. The archaeologist, in your brain, trails off about the inevitability of *future collapse*.

*

You walk the entire base of the pyramid, pausing at each serpent's head, moving your head, snake-esque, toward stone effigies. Two months from now, you will understand *future collapse*. Not now, though. Now, still rooks & moats.

*

In excavations of cenotes surrounding the archaeological site, researchers used diving equipment to explore underwater limestone shelves. They found stingray spines—ritual sacrifices to bring rain. They found bones of animals & humans with remnants of physiological stress. Indications of various flayings, tortures & mutilations only elite Maya priests preformed.

Offerings, you mouth aloud.

*

Gateway, the archaeologist said. Water: the main pathway to Xibalbá. Water comprises 70% of each human cell. Trillions of cells. Two months from now, you will understand *future collapse*. Not now, though. Now, all rooks & moats & cells.

*

You imagine your body decomposing. This decomposition becomes a leaking. Leaking until your organs & flesh mix with rain.

Your liquified-guts & rain become a pulsing river flooding underneath the Temple of Kukulcán's platform, twisting, umbilical-esque, below the smaller temple structure, pouring & splashing into the cenote below them both. Tornadic swirling continues through cenote waters into Xibalbá as rain—rain against thousands & thousands of fleshless stingrays.

Stingrays who for one moment feel your liquified guts on their slick bones & remember, *Ah, I too can float.*

Visual Invitation to Attract

if only the flesh would flake
swig its residue
be a little more than a murmur

Sandra Ruiz, *Left Turns in Brown Study*

Xibalbá (n.)

xi·bal·ba (SHə-bawl-buh)

1. : Maya underworld; where spirits go after death
2. : translations include: place of fright, place of phantoms, place of fear
    1. : some call a "dangerous place" ruled by The Lords of Xibalbá, cruel gods, trickster gods
3. : place documented in the *Popol Vuh*, the K'iche' Maya creation text
    1. : the place where the Hero Twins, Hunahpú and Xbalanqué, return from to become the Sun & Moon (See also: poem "Xibalbá :: Creation") (See also: poem "Xibalbá :: Rebirth")
    2. : the place where the Hero Twins' father and uncle were killed by The Lords of Xibalbá
4. : access through cenotes, caves or bodies of water
    1. (See also: Liquidity of Cells In Body) (See also: Tongue Of You)
5. : thin, liminal threads keeping us from the galaxies, heavens, from the supernatural (See: "Our mind has a borderline with the universe, there, where we promenade, and where tragedy resides." — Etel Adnan, *Night*, page 13)
6. : malignant invasive lobular carcinoma
7. : Red Devil
    1. (See also: Doxorubicin) (See also: Chemo Drug Eliciting Fire-Red Pee) (See: Cardiotoxicity, Nausea, Vomiting, Hair Loss, Mouth Sores) (See: Your Body Float Above You While Heaving-Vomit-Until-Your-Throat-Bleeds-&-Each-Follicle-Burn-Boils-In-Your-Scalp) (See: Did Your Chest Survive This?) (See also: What Chemo Trickster Gods)
8. : conscious state while receiving five months of chemotherapy treatment; what the body endures
    1. (See also: "Night deepens, and this is the question: Who's dreaming who? A fault-line separates us from our share." — Etel Adnan, *Night*, page 28)
9. : chest/lymph node radiation (See also: Knuckles Of Scar Tissue Forming)
10. : dry, non-elasticity of a vagina in chemo-induced menopause (See also: poem "Xibalbá :: Wilt")
11. : place of reclamation; threadbare sheen pulled back on cognition; place to return back from
    1. (See also: 3.1 above—Hunahpú and Xbalanqué's journeys in the *Popol Vuh*)
    2. (See also: poems "Xibalbá :: Holes" & "Xibalbá :: Consume") (See also: "It's good to stay in discontinuity, there/ where birds live, [...]/ we manage to bear the unbearable." — Etel Adnan, *Time*, page 22) (See also: "Something can be revealed in these moments of distraction." — Sara Ahmed, "On Being Directed," *Living a Feminist Life*, page 45)

{All the Blood Makes You Pause}

Raise your forearm. There, that's the good blood flow I am looking for. Her elevated brows. The nurse smiles under her mask. Infusion day. Again. Taxol later. First, three vials drawn from the port in the right side of your chest. Tests measure: CO2, protein, ALK Phosphatase, white blood cell count, calcium, hemoglobin, platelets, red blood cell count, potassium, glucose, & on & on. Dr. X translates results. Bloodwork. If your blood allows, you get Taxol. Never mind the neuropathy, the burning of fingertips, the rash, the shooting pains, *possibly permanent* lingers in the air. You get Taxol. How a gap changes things. *Blood work*. The nurse shakes the bloody vials. Piercing sacrifices, not just ancient things. Imperatives swarm you. Skull-faced Tlāhuizcalpantēcuhtli strikes Chalchiuhtlicue's leg. Goddess of Running Water. Blood gushes from her shin. Her eyes closed, hand uplifted to geyser as if to say, *This ain't nothing*. An alligator-meets-fish bleeds, pre-speared below her. All the blood makes you pause. Of all befores. All afters. Of skull-faced Tlāhuizcalpantēcuhtli & Running Water, who prays to the pause most? Who needs results more? You lean back in your chair, lift palm chanting, *Blood, work. Blood, work. Blood, work. Blood, work. Blood, work.*

{Deer with 20 Day Signs Attached to Body}

Reeds in one hoof, water in the other. Belly read right to left: dog, water, rabbit, deer, death. Deer, Xōchipilli's representative, young prince of flowers, what brings you here, mid squat, with monkey in your chest, alligator & wind at your feet? The flowers talk theories. Deer in belly of deer. The flowers talk in secret.

{Descent Into the Mouth of Earth Monster}

In Center, a hinge
of space, hinge
of time. Rectilinear
middles, middle of
Earth, open
hungry. I am
the figure, curved
upside down, headfirst
into teeth. I pray
to make the leap
heart-first. Heart-first
into devour.

{Among the Maize Plants}

Feed. Earth tree rises. Two ears of corn rise & bone awls rise too. Pierce an organ. Make the organ sexual. Pierce a second. What you know of autosacrifice: *willingness* & *give* must exist. All your organs feed/have fed. What you lay your body down for; how orgasm keeps your fingers less hungry at night; how you tell the awl, *wait*.

Xibalbá :: Consume

Hunahpú & Xbalanqué embrace, then leap into the fire. Here in the *Popol Vuh,* the twins resist the Lords of Xibalbá. Prior to the bonfire, the twins spoke to soothsayers, telling them to grind their bones after smolder & toss the ashes in the river. Five days later they transform into fishmen. The twins knew regeneration meant parts of them must die in Xibalbá. In the last seven sessions of radiation, the deep tissues in your armpit, left chest wall, & neck lymph nodes burn & flare inside your body. *But your skin looks great*, the radiation therapist smiles. You lay on the table, gazing up into calculating lead morphing shape to not radiate your heart or lungs & you see Hunahpú & Xbalanqué embrace. A long, patient hold before release, before the jump. Did One Death & Seven Death delight in their fiery death? Did Hunahpú & Xbalanqué smile at each other? You see them holding hands. Palm to palm. In your reflection, lasers cross the incision spanning your breast & infrared markings glow. The machine revs up. Over the intercom you hear, *Take a deep breath in. Hold your breath.* You hold. You feel the brothers stiffen, briefly, before flames completely consume.

Archive Notes #3 :: Codex Yoalli Ehēcatl, Vatican Apostolic Library, September 2022

deities of the night –   all
god
through   story.   a woman   Notice
what   I offer
the importance of
Another exposed
death   .
curious   architects
designing

vivid   sharp
living,
touched   surface
a bladder
worn symbols   partial
bleed
away.   the underworld   ;   goddess of the underworld
present here.

central
supernatural
movement   besides   wonder
outlines   the spirit   outlines

Alive   so much

vibrant –   deity

disrupted

uneven

a bit uneven
cut uneven. I

look

worn been burned
through to the light

Vision Offerings

Turquoise. A god's heart, opaque in minerality, in stratification of what-we-
think-to-be-blue, of what-we-think-to-be-green, then transformation. Body
as concentric casings of bodies. How the Maya understand hydrousness.
Constituent of. Color said to connect heaven & Earth: fibrous as a hue.
The hue, my gods, the hue.

Glassy, glassy
innards
of box-nosed
serpents swarm.

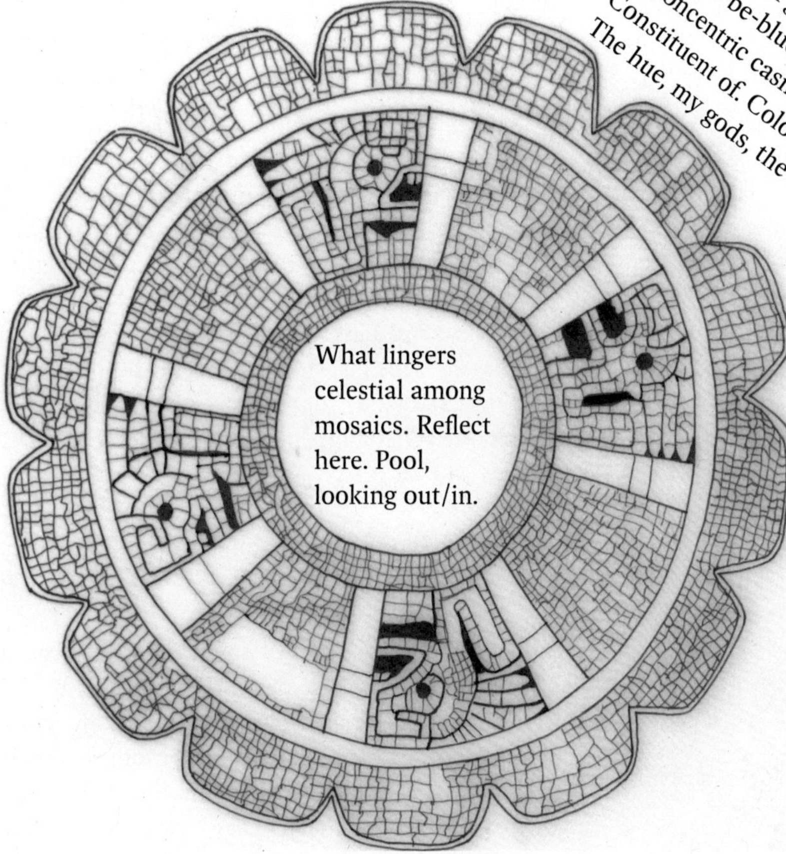

Pieces. What begins
in shards, reforms. A slice
a type of trace. Even comets
wound the sky, briefly.

Break down *recovery*, in the mouth, heart, hands. *Taken* transcribed to science. In the Temple of the Warriors, Chac Mool before the serpents, laid back yet alert. Bench. *What taken from.* Knees up, hands on your abdomen, face turned ninety degrees out from the temple. You, part speculation, part sacrificial altar, part belly—a bowl to place the heart & blood inside. Your identity enigmatic—& the *whats, whens, hows* mount in your silence. Our webbing-tissues-of-silence. Gaps construct questionnaire after questionnaire: & I'm tired, so tired, of being tested. You see what most do not see: prediction. Our eyes tunnel centuries: you here, me there. A trace a type of constellation. Let us connect our stars in galaxies of flesh & stone. Time, most relentless invitation. I see you seeing me. I praise you, your kin, as kin.

{All the Blood Makes You Pause}

As a child, you twisted a hanging plant on a dare. Twisted & twisted until the ceramic holder broke over your foot. Blood soaked your jelly shoes in the run home. You hid behind the bathroom door until your mother found you. Twelve stitches. You remember warmth between your toes, along with the throbbing gash. Xochiquétzal, young goddess of moon, can't she see the bat above her holds a heart? Blood floods her face. Warm in bifurcated torrent; who you try to impress; who laughs & who's left wanting; what trees sprout from your ribs.

{All the Blood Makes You Pause}

You bled first at church. Down in the basement bathroom, below the altar, rolling toilet paper around your hand, measuring the lining of your underwear. Insistence of blood in a girl's body. Threat of leaking though. Threat of the boy you desired pointing at your blood-soaked ass. Threat of smelling iron in pubic hair & the jokes across one-arm desks. Girls throwing ketchup-soaked pads down the halls like hand grenades. You rarely thought of sacrifice then, even in the crucifix bathroom. Now, your fingers trace Smoke Eye, in hummingbird costume, his last appearance in the ritual sequence. His supernatural journey through blood, to become, transformed. How many of your rituals require blood? What happens when the blood stops?

{All the Blood Makes You Pause}

Chemo forces you into menopause, so you notice blood. How when buying a new Honda CRV & suddenly Honda CRVs drop from the sky. Same color too. Color is important. You notice blood like that. Blood spilling, then not. You who becomes bloodless outside the body. You who no longer bleeds from between your legs. You who no longer is able to reproduce. You *childless*. You *crone*. You who did not produce a child which *is your purpose*. You who lineage from sacrifice. Jose who worked at the chicken plucking plant. Snapping necks. Linda who took the fists. How a bruise consumes tendons, filament, organs, the underside of flesh, makes a person tender behind bone. Evelyn who inherited $25k from her brother Willis. Farm-family mentality, only for Bernard to buy a tin roof for the motel. The *pin pin pin* before the thunderstorms—her head in her hands. Her veins running through yours. No more future veins.

Xibalbá :: Creation

A ballcourt exists in Xibalbá. A great ballcourt below the Great Ballcourt above. Chichén Itzá means: *Mouth at the well of Itzá*. Fitting. All the things you shove your head & hands into with a desire to echo.

*

Reading about the acoustics, you planned to stand at the South Temple end, make Chris stand at the North Temple & clap. Today the rain plans otherwise. You wander the site unable to hear the tour guide, let alone wet clapping hands. Staring up at the stone scoring rings, you imagine the Hero Twins.

*

Pok-Ta-Tok ring. Chichén Itzá. June 2022. One month before diagnosis.

*

One Death & Seven Death in Xibalbá hear Hunahpú & Xbalanqué playing with their father's Pok-Ta-Tok equipment above. You imagine the twins bumping the rubber ball off their shoulders & hips into the 20-foot hoop. You imagine the twins playing even in this downpour, or snapping their godly fingers & poof, no rain. How the twins on the ballcourt enrage One Death & Seven Death. How the lords of Xibalbá cheat at Pok-Ta-Tok, how they murdered Hunahpú & Xbalanqué's father & uncle (also twins). How the Lords of Xibalbá lure Hunahpú & Xbalanqué down to the underworld to trick & kill them too. *Who does my playing offend?* You want to clap your hands.

*

All gods. Hunahpú & Xbalanqué were gods, not humans. How even our gods bicker like us. Fight like us. Kill like us. Destroy like us. *What do I destroy?*

*

Skip to the end. You cannot. You want to clap your hands.

*

Over a *game*. The idea of *game* charges you; you feel electrical; you pulsate. Imagine being dangled, punchline-esque, by a higher power that you don't understand & doesn't understand you. Being played. All those danglings. *What do I dangle*?

*

The twins throw the ballgame to survive. They keep surviving. They survived: the Dark House, Knives House, Cold House, Jaguar House, Fire House, then get decapitated in the Bat House (only Hunahpú). After beheading, Xbalanqué swaps Hunahpú's head for a gourd with brains

> (Pause. The image of Scarecrow. The first time you watched the *Wizard of Oz*, you felt sympathetic to the Wicked Witch of the East. You knew Dorothy stole those damn ruby slippers & being young before Maguire wrote *Wicked* in '95, which you didn't read until the 2000s, you sense witches being mistreated for their green skin wasn't unlike growing up Mexican in Alden, IA in the 80s. Of course. You so full of seeds & pulp. *What have you done to simply survive?*)

to play another round of Pok-Ta-Tok. This time, the twins win against the Xibalbáns.

*

The story does not end here. Skip to the end. You cannot. You want to clap your hands.

*

The Great Ball Court with serpent's head & Pok-Ta-Tok ring in distance.
Chichén Itzá. June 2022. One month before diagnosis.

*

Ends make you prickly. You call all endings into suspicion. When a story ends. When a life ends. Connective tissues in between. When do you know the end is *the end*? Perhaps when the tour guide says, *Okay, everyone find your way back to the bus*. Perhaps when listening to version after version of the *Popol*

Vuh & your heart races from connection/disconnection simultaneously & you get interrupted. You pause the story. A pause as a type of echo.

*

Perhaps when you travel to the Yucatán to recognize some semblance of your own lineage on carved limestone. To hear hands clapping that only you can hear.

*

Skip to the end. Hunahpú leaves Xibalbá to become the Sun. Xbalanqué, the Moon. Their journey prepares the world for humans to be created. Skip to the end. You cannot. You type knowing you cannot. Ends make Xibalbá tactile, not subversive. The thing the editor wants you to say but you're not saying. The part everyone chomps at the bit for, the part you can't give. You look into the Well of Itzá. The hole telescopes into infinity.

*

As the bus drives away from Chichén, your knees & forearms cover in goosebumps. You imagine the twins on the ballcourt just before One Death & Seven Death summon them. The shadow of the rings crossing their faces. *Play like us too.* You look up at the sun passing behind clouds. *Hunahpú.* You softly put your palms together & clap.

Ecogodliness

You trace sundogs [Emerson on mind again & yellowing
words on yellowing pages] imbibing

permeability. Your eyes lick atmosphere. A semblance
of washing impermanence. What refuses

to clot. Anywhere that resembles a bloody something
to clot. [All you still refuse to acknowledge: *to to to*.] All hacks

& limbs of you; yet save the gore for another
witness. [& we do witness.] Sundog. Preposition. Noun.

Of all the nouns you sift through, it's the *somethings*
that haunt the most. Their precipice of acts

acting: a whisper heard behind the ear, until you realize:
the ear itself whispering. How the sweeping of concentric circles

[damn you Emerson] wears on the body: how a gerund masks
its own verbness with desire to noun [how the nouning

yes the nouning becomes the lust]. Aren't we all a type of blaze
placed haphazardly [yet designingly] besides another blaze?

How origins tempt us: a type of reminder—all fleeting
from & all shining iridescent *to*—brief, now briefer still.

Xibalbá :: Desire

“260 days in the Maya calendar & at one time 260 bones in the human body.” The tour guide explains outside the Group of a Thousand Columns. Almost-exactness. We begin with 270 bones at birth. We evolve by fusing. We evolve to 206 bones. Somewhere in between: a sacred number. At Chichén Itzá, the guide takes down his mask & my brother’s cheek bones, ocular structures, nose, & mouth inhabit another person. *How many other faces wear my face?* Joe changed his legal name from *Jose Francisco Zamora Jr.* How lineage of a “Jr.” culled him. *What culls him now? What culls me?* I want to hug this guide; pretend he’s Joe. Pretend he’s a family member I desire him to be. A tap behind my breastbone. A dream dissipating before sleep. *Desire brought me here.* Mind lost in reactions. How the guide connects the numbers 13, 20, 52, and 260 to specific anatomical parts of the human body. “26 in the spine.” Maya nine-month year represents birth. *Tōnalpōhualli, all sacredness, all cosmos.* How European conquistadors realized their Julian calendars flawed & used Mesoamerican calendars to create Gregorian calendars. “Flaws” of empire. *My own flawedness.* By the bus, I tell Aapo, “You look like my brother.” He hugs me. I worship desire. Hand on his vertebral column, I begin counting.

Earthly Rhythms

You don't speak Spanish. You don't speak Nahautl. You study the Codex regardless. Blemishes compound you. How a year ago these facts shamed you. Inherited traumas sag in your guts. {You remember your internalized-oppression training. Facilitator guiding, *Imagine a world with no oppression.* Interior swell.} Now, you welcome cracks, cell by cell sighing out from flesh, from metastasized ______, from the five-inch scar where breast tissue once lived, from baldness, from two years until your hair might touch your chin, from swollen eyes where eyelashes fell out.

*

You ache. All of you sucked out of marrow. Greedy world too languished & loving of women's pain. {Resist *dismissive*. Term too gentle for the tearing.} Cancer forces you into menopause. 85% of menstruating people experience menopause symptoms. Society's "high cultural tolerance for women's suffering." You text your friend about pap smears. Response: *Why can't we just have some sort of hi-def screen we walk behind, fully clothed, that tells us everything we need to know?* You laugh. {Discomfort in this laugh; interrogate both the laugh & the discomfort.} Response: *This screen probably exists, but men stashed it away or burned the blueprints. No money in healthy women. Unbecoming of capitalism.*

*

You once believed health lived inside you. All mistakes in believing.

*

You write *cancer* next to *codex* on journal pages. Step back to breathe in the unsaid here

_____. Here too _____. {Do not give your full self to the poem. The poem is full enough.} You rupture—the way a fissure forms in Earth's surface. Promise of release.

*

In *Doomstead Days*, Teare reveals how a body with chronic illness intertwines the Anthropocene, our obsessions, the biotariat. Biological hemispheres & landscapes of us. Us impacting earthly rhythms. Our bodies as earthly rhythms. A volcano might be misinterpreted as blemish. Promise of release.

*

In the Codex Yoalli Ehēcatl, you see fragments of the Tōnalpōhualli. One deer pierced with an arrow next to one dead deer—how the supernatural inhabits daily practice—the bloodshed before the deer's eyes close. Inherited practices. You pierced & squirming? Quiet & gray? Shedding blood or slowly closing your eyes? {Unsure of your own answers.} The calendrical in the fluids, flesh, cells. You see Stipe Eye's journey beginning on the blue road. You see divination. Your heart a type of conjure. The echocardiograms tell the oncologist the chemo isn't frying your aortic valve while hearing cadence in the swift *whaawhamp whaawhamp whaawhamp*. A ventricle relaxes; a tricuspid value opens. Reminders how the body sings despite.

*

You kneel to the Nine Lords of Night. {Not to beg, to gain vantage point. To understand cycles.} All omens & fortunes out of your hands. You etch each letter *t-r-a-n-s-f-o-r-m-a-t-i-o-n* on 14 white pills. {All the sonnets you swallow.} Feel the healing in your stomach for four days after the Red Devil.

All the devils you let in. Devils at the door.

What stomps around inside you, not always guest.

*

{Do not give your full self to the poem. The poem is full enough.}

The poem hungers. You hunger.

*

The Codex reminds you of oblivion—*before-before,* when your first form sculpted in comet tails. Dust falling to Earth, nestling particle by particle by particle inside your ancestors, womb after womb until you tumble—song in valves. You at your own door. Galaxy's sparkle between teeth. A minuscule devil gestating minuscule devils.

Hunger Sonnet

I lose my fingers inside my solar plexus :: Worm
too deep—*A sense of knowing*, I whisper :: You

murmur back sucking on my knuckle bones :: Our stomach
expands, our stomach contracts :: *Why do you hide* :: Spinal

nerves connect organs to our brain :: sympathetic
nervous system :: our stomach uncoils :: *Not satiated*, you say,

preparation, making room to breathe in the discomfort of you :: You
understand your work :: I miss my thumbs, my radiocarpal

joints hinge :: You coil tighter, *I harp organs—instrument you,*
you think you so delicate, you add pressure :: *Aren't I* :: I choke

& we release :: *Ouroboros, eat. Nasty liar*. You treble, a choir
multivoicing out :: *I am serpent born* :: No longer

distinguishable :: *In you :: Of you* :: Our loud feast. I stare
at the semicircle of bones littering the ground.

Serpent's Head, Jaguar Temple Chichén Itzá.
June 2022. One month before diagnosis.

Xibalbá :: Minuscule Devils

What fuses in the dark?

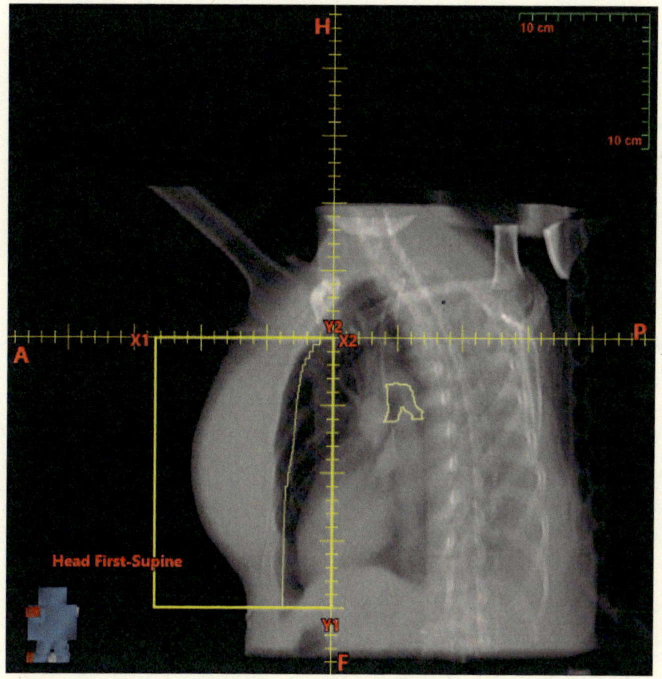

206 bones watch.

Xibalbá :: Unbearable

I learn quick to play the part. Smiling-Patient gets tentative questions, eye contact, emails answered. Surgeons love Smiling-Patient.

*

Smiling-Patient always rates pain below 5 on the scale of 0-10, because Smiling-Patient understands that numbers 6 or above are false-bottom answers that fall & fall & fall. Numbers & voices trickle out of earshot.

*

Smiling-Patient knows when her doctor says, *You shouldn't be in that much pain,* you just keep smiling.

*

How the world trains me. *Let let let.*

All the ways I must untrain myself. Often, too, from myself.

*

A phrase such as *self-advocate* seems powerful until I'm left-breastless, naked in an exam room. A surgeon finger pokes in my armpit. I wince & crocodile-tear while the med student in clinical rotation steps back, adverts her eyes, & the words *This cannot hurt* separate & slither at my feet.

Neither Smiling-Patient or self-advocate appear.

I'm left with inverted mountain of unsaids & a bloating shame. (How often unable.) (How when often unable, memory gets packed up, put away, clayed into antimemory. *Survive, survive.*)

*

Just below hairs of Smiling-Patient, I linger.

Dissect each of my trillion cells to find nano-versions of me wailing multiverses of decibels, caked in cytoplasm, DNA, lysosome, Gogli apparatus. A concerto of sorts.

*

Wailing never interested me, of course until uncorked, blowhole-esque, unable to be stuffed back into my lungs.

All the wailing I ignore.

Selfish shit, to ignore wailing until I wailed. How often the gaps (cognitive, anatomical, metaphysical) constitute me.

*

The world wails & I look away.

In the tale of La Llorona, when the ghost roams water in mourn of the children she drowned, did she mourn the children's death or her act? Did she play a part? Did she invest too cruelly in antimemory?

*

A wail becomes a prayer as an act of absolution from what-we-cannot-bear-to-acknowledge.

I, Smiling-Patient, unbearable to myself.

Message to the Skeletal Earth Goddess

The Duende separate from the muse & the angel. Bodily. Inheritance. Tlazōlteōtl, all passages through you. What passes. Chest cracked open. Your delicate keep. Your riotous discard. What stirs you. Sours each jagged seam. I obsess with interiority. Rattles: ribs separate in hollowed-out breastbone. I, in your cage—low crepitus of bone-on-bone. What if descent is a lie? Only cracks into other dimensions. Portals. Flesh & terrestrial alike. Duende shaken loose. Another form of energy. Form of elegy. Busting open. Reconfigures inside out.

Hint: An Ars Poetica Triptych on Relationship

*

mine the word. reveal me to me. belly
unhides sunken spots, the under-under,
out of out spray of, unable to hold
hints of tendrils of brain. hint
all the spouts Let me

*

Between the words *body*
& *braiding*—all our betweenness—

a litany of *be*. What burns under
the soft folds. What cranial mechanisms

kiss into flame from an unknown specter
or god or happen-stance collision. A tally

exists here—in the gaps—you look at empty
through a magnifying glass. You compile a list

of b-words to find_______. To find?
What compounds inside you

tethers, tethers with intimacy. You
bemoan in all this intimacy.

*

Always beginning in a body. A start, as *to be—known* a place to dwell—place where comforts haunt: a comingling. Crack a word & what spills forth. Mine the mess. Soak the mess with napkins & gobble those suckers back in your mouth. No one baptizes anyone anymore. *Good gracious*, says your devilish tongue. Always an origin of firstborns, of birth, of wombing. Let's all lick the apples & put them back on the shelf scarred with our teeth marks. *I got a little sumpin sumpin in me.* Flesh of a thing—say *dressing*, say *what holds interior*. You know, *You've done this before. The saying.* Oh, the comforts comforting. If you want to write about the heart of anything, pluck out the organ & resist naming. Study the thud & let the thumping collapse you. You must become a keeper. K writes about bears—metaphors for feminist discourse—in delicious poems burgeoning the ecstatic. K keeps bears now. K keeps bears to ward off toxic masculinity. An antidote. [You know what you keep just to sleep at night.] [Naughty little keeper, you.] You must become a keeper. Keeper of sinew. Keeper of ribs, an understudy of bone. In your obsession with forming, ask your own chicken/egg inquires: *Poem or possibility of poem*? You wicked little *possibility*. All this *possibility* to arrive at the *page* [insert physical or mental location instead] [all the damn *insteads*] less broken, more ferocious, more fangs, more spittle. You want to wrap yourself in a fang. Fang out. Be fang. You know who created the lexicon for the devil. You know how the poem wants it all tender & all brutal at once. Greedy bitch. You & the poem...want want want want want.

Dilution Effect

Writing can shift the mechanism of time by changing the record, then changing the event.

Mei-Mei Berssenbrugge, *A Treatise on Stars*

Murmuration (n.) (v.)

mur.mur̄.ra.tion (murr-muh-RAY-shuhn)

1. : starling flock
2. : literary (v): act of murmuring; utterance of low continuous sounds
3. : named for its sound—a low murmur from soft flight calls
    1. (See also: A Thousand Wings Beating) (See also: poem "Xibalbá :: Rebirth")
4. : *my ear inches from the Codex Yoalli Ehēcatl: murmuration feed*
5. : flock of, flock to (See also: Flocking Inside My Bones)
6. : unlike V formations in birds, murmurations are unique flocks providing no aerodynamic advantage
    1. (See also: We Don't Need Purpose To Fly) (See also: Innately Keeping)
7. : a homecoming (See also: Ancestral Swarm) (See also: poem "Undulation :: Plate 8")
8. : migratory gathering (See also: Muscle Of You) (See also: section titles of this book)

1. : purpose for: increased numbers phenomenology to reduce predatory impact on individuals (See also: this section's title), exchange of information, visual display to entice, dusk centric (See also: Your Own Dusky Heart)

9. : what refuses legibility (See: Guts Of You) (See: Violent Language) (See: Un-ness) (See: Cognitive Wilding/ Organic Wilding)
10. : pluralness
11. : saying, *trust the instincts; now move we*

Undulations :: Plate 39

{11 Human Footprints on the 11TH Page of the Ritual Sequence}

Trace a number. I'm tracing. Do you remember in little league. Yes, I played on the Alley Cats & mom took scissors to my hair. Yes, the pixie cut fiasco. I learned to slide into first base. Your jersey. Do you remember? Number 11. I remember each one sticking to my back on humid nights. 11 became your favorite number. Still is. Whenever I play roulette, I place chips on number 11. Do you believe in attachments? Like you & me? More like tucked away inside the folds of medial prefrontal cortex. Like you & me? More like a poltergeist who only haunts houses of flesh. Only if the poltergeist & I are friends. You must be right. II am. II am.

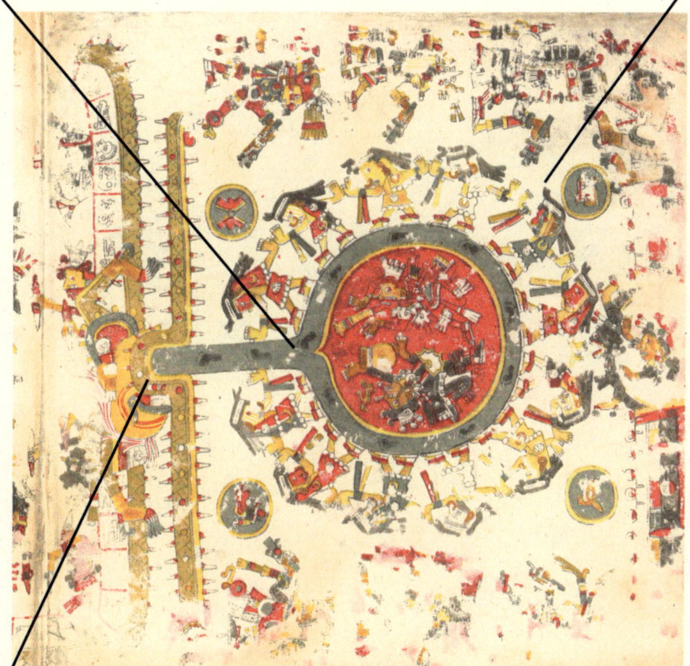

{12 Female Spirits Dance}

Cihuateteo, the "Divine Women," mothers
who died giving birth, who died
in the act of creation. Childbirth, a battle
in the eyes of the Aztecs. You move
sinuous, head bowed, thumbs in touch
you warriors, you fallen into skeletal
faces, into claws instead of fingernails,
you ring around the red Quetzalcōātl
& the sojourner's falling wombed
in tear, inside your orbicular glide,
glide, glide of steps. Churn. What you
orb in ceremony. Rhythm frozen between
grass & movement & wind & deer. I am
wound by you; you who scratch
upon my eardrum; you who coat
heavy fog on my retinas: a vision
of fallopian tubes echoing empty, empty.

{Jaws of the Earth Monster, Wide, Wider}

Step into the sharpness. Why must we test our own becoming? We mistake the blades for. We mistake the sharpness for. Let us remember all that sprouts from soil, seeps from sea. Loosen the fang. Lean into the potential loss. Place your body in the gap. Pray for the consumption.

Ecogodliness

The gutter drools a slow drip
& this baptism of storm crawls

back into lips of clouds, licks
tonsils of sky to esophagus

of atmosphere—you comb
wet grasses with fingers & palms.

Soon. Reduction to damp, reduction
to dry. What beloved we beyond

a summoning of desires: rain
to soak the drought, drought

to drain the flood, flood finch's song
to unravel the funnel cloud's hatch

across a prairie horizon. Psalm
exists here—in gaps between want

& fathom. You unknow the robin's
egg bundles in nest or smashes at tree's

rooted base. *Know.* Palmistry sews within
your pericardium. *Unknow*: a giving

of sinew & self over to the elements. Be
element as element. *Unlearn*: any

birthrights: all passages. Psalm exists
where wind awakens bark & branch —

to beckon a wave of limbs, forest
full of chorus, *Here here, belong with us.*

Xibalbá :: Ritual

_____ _____, (*birthdate*). I slide my left arm out of the pink hospital wrap before the technician says *Good*. Twenty-five days of_____ _____ , (*birthdate*) & the response, *Good, that's you*. Each step of cancer treatment becomes its own type of ritual. With chemo: *Say your name & birthdate*, Heparin to clean the port, bloodwork, the hot blanket, Decadron & antinausea IVs first, the dietitian's *Are you eating*?, tonguing my mouth sores while I lie about not eating spicy food, then the Red Devil, later Taxol, constructs of time disintegrating, beeping monitors, more Heparin, the *See you next weeks*. Now with radiation: day-after-day of *No I have not fallen since yesterday, No I have not come into contact with someone who has Covid since yesterday*, waiting room florescence, *We're ready for you*, bare chest, hospital wrap, locker key, my name my name my name, my birthdate my birthdate my birthdate, bare chest, laying on the table with the head-neck-shoulder pillow molded to my form, the country music station, thinking about my dislike of country music but feeling like a shit because it's not my space, the technicians closing the two-feet thick radiation door, the interior conversation about keeping my eyes closed or open while the machine runs, closing my eyes, opening my eyes, the intercom voice saying *Breathe in & hold your breath*, closing my eyes, opening my eyes, counting second-by-second on each breath-hold, *one one-thousand, two one-thousand, three one-thousand*, worrying a shallow breath will melt my innards, worrying too deep of a breath will melt my innards, sound of the machine starting & stopping reminds me of Ripley using the power loader to fight the xenomorph queen in *Aliens*, looking into the gray-brown lead to memorize the shape of the anvil & thinking of all that hammers me today & how I'd rock that power loader suit too—make those metal hips shake shake shake— & Sigourney Weaver & I create a choreographed dance where we lock massive wrench-hands & twirl & twirl & twirl until my motion sickness kicks in & I throw up in front of Sigourney & she laughs saying *I still throw up on merry-go-rounds* & we take off the power loaders & head to Urban Artifact to drink sour beers & talk-laugh about all the monstrosities itching to burrow inside us—itching to break us but can't.

Remembering Etel Adnan While Filling Out the Ohio Power of Attorney Before the Mastectomy

Adnan wrote, *My own disappearance*
followed [...] Acts in preparation
of a world without me. Care
amounting to a pinprick hole
no one notices. My laugh
becoming space
to fill. Cumulous. *[...] a cloud*
that found me [...]. Malleable
form. Filling. Who fills
ether? Always a who. Always filling
a gap beyond gape: [...] *sitting*
in a garden. A rainbow always
in never-fill of sky, brief, then—

Message to the Goddess of Running Water

Skull-faced Tlāhuizcalpantēcuhtli impales you. Chalchiuhtlicue, Goddess of the East. Tlāhuizcalpantēcuhtli, placed West. Directions, too, in conflict. War inside creates war outside. All the *outsides*. All the *insides*. Where you flow. Blood contains 83% water. Blood contains 55% plasma. Plasma contains 92% water. Tlāhuizcalpantēcuhtli stabs. & we all wail. Aquatic embodiment. Deity of floods. Storms bound in you. Fourth sun. Your stoic face—knowing sacrifice. Knowing all blood delivers. Once, my lizard brain. Once, my smooth babe-chest. Once, my fertile maize stalk. Now, liquidity—lack of liquidity. Reservoirs in my platelets quiver.

Plaything

Before "Mexico Asks Vatican for Temporary Return of Ancient Indigenous Manuscripts" which included the Codex Yoalli Ehēcatl. Before the Pope denies Mexican President Andrés Manuel López Obrador. Before "difficult anniversaries." Before the Spanish government rejected López Obrador, "the arrival of the Spanish 500 years ago to present-day Mexican lands cannot be judged in light of contemporary considerations." Before the Codex Yoalli Ehēcatl's renamed to *Codex Borgia*. Before living in the Vatican Apostolic Library. Before Alexander von Humbolt rummaged through the effects of Carinal Stefan Borgia after his death in 1805. Before Cardinal Borgia acquired the Codex from neighbors, the Giustiniani family. Before the Guistiniani family handed the Codex to their servants. Before the servants gave the Codex to their children as *a plaything*. Before lit matches. Before the singeing pages. Before fires put out. Before *plaything*. Before water damage. Before the scars of mistreatment. Before *play*. Before *thing*. Before the *best-preserved*. Before *surviving*. Before *painted without hint of European influence*. Before surviving. Before pre-Conquest style. Before *surviving*:

*

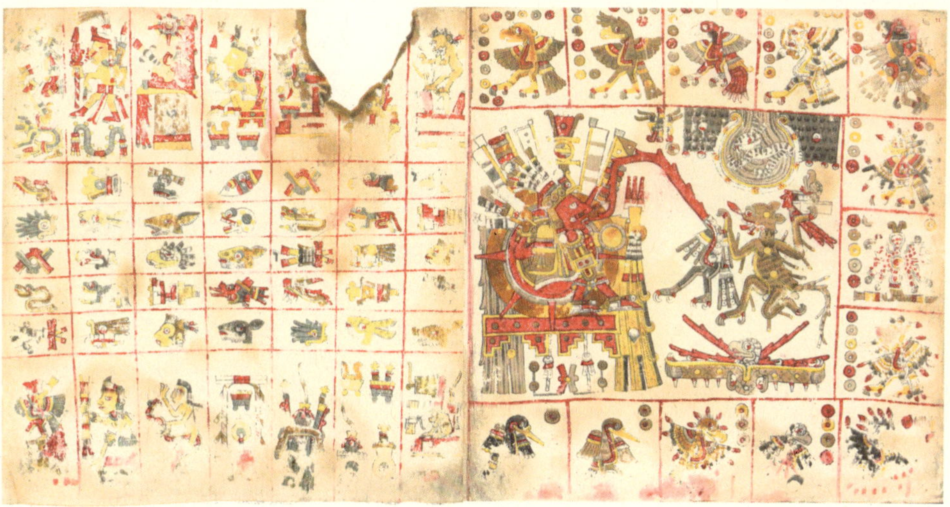

My ancestors attached 14 strips of animal skin, end-to-end. Trimmed to 27 cm. Sectioned into 39 equal-sized leaves. Screen-folded. Applied white lime-plaster for painting. Used mineral & vegetable pigments. Painted. Painted gods. Mesoamerican rituals. Mesoamerican divinations. Painted visual representations of the Tōnalpōhualli. Painted calendrically. Painted ceremonially through shared religious systems. Painted for auguries & oracles predicting patterns through interactions of physical worlds & supernatural worlds.

Yoalli as *night*. Ehēcatl as *spirit of air*. Yoalli Ehēcatl as *Night Wind*—deity, primordial parent to human & god creation.

Nuances of belief.

*

Now, we guess at the names for deities drawn. We guess *Nahuatl*, yet language unknown. Documents taken. Voices taken. Exact region: unknown. Exact timeframe: unknown. Painters remain nameless. Unknown. Rituals: only guesses. Unknown.

Unknowns bead along my hairline. When I read about my own lineage as a colonizer's *plaything*: an engulfed puff of air slides along my breastbone to ribs via cartilage, to protect the heart & lungs, to whisper in preparation, *Such aches born inside you.*

Xibalbá :: If-ness

The toad speaks to me. Chin bloat, extending

& I too long for extension. The playwright warns of death

inside each performance; this too, a performance

so too, a death. What must die to become. Toad song

a continuance that too, ends, just as the stipules

Brand maps—tiny amygdalae inside amygdalae—we

all clerks clerking, authors authoring. The novelist

touches my forearm, *Gather them. Let them touch you*

to channel their energy to you. What verdancy

what moisture-ridden croaks my body might make

if surveillance turns me inside out, if the possible

[yet not inevitable] returns returns returns—enters

my cells again, disguised as my cells. If indecipherable

authoring. If-ness a type of death—quietly, quietly.

A Story for the Cosmos: A Tetraptych

::

God N, you stand, Pawahtuun, at the four corners of Earth. Manifestation of First Father. Primordial. All the absent fathers, invisible; the desires & prayers never answered.

Cosmos pliable between your palms. When you thought to support the sky, did you think of me, knocking at your turtle shell armor, whispering,

I too carry worlds on my back,

squatting in angles, looking out

to undo edges.

::

A trace is a love story
of fatherless children
of women who birth
themselves, who cord
umbilical serpents & make homes
in their own ribs.
The cosmos tips
when I bow. Cosmos
shakes when I tussle
these soft bones
shimmy shimmy
into a verdancy so dazzling
Earth's axis quakes.

::

You created the world—then not out of miracles, transformed to snails, raptors, the alligator's back. Itzam Ahiin, body of the Earth. You became World. Some say you survived as *Mam*. Licentious. Lewd & undignified. I love you in your promiscuity. All my misdeeds seeking altars. Daughter of my own bloodline, of my filthy & succulent heart. How the Maya relish in your buffoonery. How once I buffooned for many, maybe even you, with a promise of fatherhood. I grow weary of chromosomes. I relinquish now. What incongruency of ancient clowning to First Father. The ancient Maya believed in over a dozen primary gods & goddesses. In disguises. How you parade in one mask, then wear another. How the terrestrial mimics the celestial. Each god playing dress up, makes me feel less exposed.

::

I touch my belly button.

I too hold possession in folds of my body. I too create the living rope, to tether the supernatural world to the natural world—

I speak of birth after birth.

Archive Notes #4 :: Codex Yoalli Ehēcatl, Vatican Apostolic Library, September 2022

plates cascade spine in cloud
flooding out
. This brown makes me

restored
love vertical light
something punctured.
■ look through this hole, remnants of the other side, soft red line
results faded
erasure feels haunting as bleed
as around the mouth
mark s
Love another seam strategically binding
lines
pencil mark
oblong cutting
the dead hole a shield, looking
on other
marks
I am awe I am this document.
I am the relic.
upside down

separated foretelling my future; inverted person,
eyes

rest

out of death's

journey

arranged

Xibalbá :: This

You gather all the places of fright
in one gelatinous tendril of your brain—

hold, if possible to hold, *this* type of thinking
for only a millisecond, then release. You train

yourself   for any concept of 'under'
when the world (you correct your own singularity

& shake your head knowing just how meta & ridiculous
this inner all is) world/s perch above. In all this perching,

this opening—   of-eyelids, this scrub-your-armpits-
with-soap-then-wash-between-vaginal-flaps, *this*
latte-swigging-get-your-ass-online-answer-a-fucking-email-
or-a-thousand-   then-take-a-shit-in-a-stall-
with-two-squares-of-toilet-paper-&-you-can't-even-ask-
the-person-beside-you-cause-you're-in-a-basement-
cause-your-old-ass-building-staggers-restrooms-

by-gender-on-every-other-fucking-floor-&-as-you-dig-
Kleenex-from-your-pocket-to-wipe-you-think-   how-constructs-
like-gender-are-designed-to-oppress-then-wipe-then-work-work-
cause-*work-is-all-that-matters*-is-ground-into-your-brain-
cause-you-got-the-bootstrap-metaphor-shoved-in-your-throat-
a-throat-already-overflowing-gorging-seeping-if-one-more-person-tells-
you-*you-work-so-hard*-so-help-us-all-   we-pretend-that-any-
of-*this*-fucking-matters-when-our-bodies-hit-rigor-
mortis-when-it-costs-two-grand-to-set-a-body-on-fire-
to-cremate-who's-gonna-pay-to-burn-your-bones-
do-you-even-have-two-grand-   you-paid-
the-vet-$800-to-cremete-Sherlock-damn-
he-was-a-good-but-neurotic-Shepherd-   you-miss-
how-he-talked-back-cry-cry-poems-hate-*this*-when-you-cry-you-
can-always-stop-here-stop-reading-stop-thinking-stop-brain-
activity-stop-*this*-finality-of-stop-when-speaking-about-the-brain-
pauses-you-*this*-kidding-*this*-   not-stop-   never-stop-you-think-
of-all-*this-this*-pauses-you-   you-pause-on-orca-whales-vultures-
over-the-woods-behind-your-house-   the-fact-you-own-a-house-
after-18-years-living-in-the-Alden-Motel-   pauses-you-slivers-you
        you-*you-of-moonlight-in-daylight*-
you-flesh-blister-burnt-radiation-machine-sculpted-gauge-of-capacity-you-

you-pause-on-

capacity-of-rats-to-withstand-tranquilizers-then- grocery-shop-

&-hope-

no-one-coughs-on-you-cause-covid-is-still-a-thing-we-pretend-

is-not-a-thing- feed-your-dogs-lick-your-wounds-

masturbate-to-Agatha-Christie-novels-lay-in-bed-for-twenty-minutes-

before-peeing— *this-this.*

Yeah, Xibalbá. You shake Xibalbá

like a rattle. Place Xibalbá under your pillow

to save for another eye-opening, millisecond perch

of cells, of tissues, to hold *this.* *This-this* rattles in skull's midnights.

{From the Blue Vessel Emerges
a Dark & Foamy Substance}

{Enclosure Formed by the Body
of the Goddess of Death}

From a curious substance, animated creatures. Winds. Winds who display characteristics of Quetzalcóatl. What emerges from the vessel of you. Shells stacking. What nesting-doll godliness inside you. Creatures who leak from your pores, your hair follicles, webbing between your fingers. Miniature feathered serpents born in your cochlea, slip through your tympanic membrane, down your ear canal to shimmy & climb up your helix. In chorus, the creatures sing back into the tunnel of you, *Dawn keeps here. Open. Dawn. Open soon. Open. Open.*

A ritual sequence begins in a goddess' body, a female body. A supernatural journey. Protagonist must pass through the goddess' jaws, her cranium to enter. She holds the sojourner in a gate of her spine, her ribs, her vertebra, her organs, her blood, her tendons, her muscles. *Body work.* All coils/recoils inside you. All you let pass through the layers of you; ghosts who linger too long in your subterrane, ghosts who ignite the flush of your cheeks. The *who* & *who* of your cranium, your thumping veins, your expanding pupils. Yet, she is the Goddess of Death. You wonder about the form of her. To string a body like barbed wire. Temptation or warning? Siren or storm? All inaccurate binaries. Her innards munch on all the dichotomies. All you hold in your guts. What you absorb. What you rebirth. What you long to spit right back out.

{Intertwined Starry Wind Serpents Spitting Out Wind Figures}

Using throat to guide. Trachea as passage as birth canal. To the next section of journey. To the next page for reader. Snakes don't use as much oxygen as humans. The right lung of a snake is large, elongated with one small left lung, or no left lung at all. Sac-like organs. Sacs share the chest cavity with the heart. The heart sits in the pericardium, another sac. How have you filled your sacs? What have you used your breath for? How down in our lungs, we build & build.

Inner

Our psyches resemble the bordertowns [...] Nothing happens in the "real" world
unless it first happens in the images in our heads

- Gloria Anzaldúa, "Towards a New Consciousness," *Borderlands/La Frontera*

You wrote of communal ground, prepare
beyond culture to unite us. All to hold us, bind
us, Gloria. Awareness of situation before inner
change. Inner change before societal change. I do
not mistake this for an equation. To develop

unencumbered, we must understand our own
split: from history, from language, from each of our faces—
the situation: intentionality behind the dominate
white culture's thoughts & actions to cull us. Realness
of our fabrication of real. Pock holes in the real to remake

the real. If we ask the llama to explain their relationship
to the herd. Silence. Someone thinks *sumpter animal.*
Someone thinks *beast of burden*. In the high alpines
of the Andes, the cousin vicuña moves at night among
steep slopes & festuca, continues to resist domestication.

Ask the vicuña, *Who do you serve*? Silence. Someone
mistakes the lack of sound for acquiescence. Someone
labels a wild thing *sacred*. Someone labels a wild thing
dangerous. Someone doesn't like the use of *animal*
or *thing* associated with their personhood. Someone

wants more *animality*, less *human*. Collapse the word
human into its embodied history of colonized with-
holding meant to deteriorate a body not white. I label
myself *animal*. Reach knuckles & wrists inside my throat
to pull & gather all the gutturals within my tissues. I wonder

who labels me *dangerou*s now. A word is a bordertown. Belief
in vocabulary means we carve ourselves out of plurality. Town
before the town. Outer terrains sculpt from inner
terrains. A mouth held shut still resides in a cerebrum firing—
thinking & voluntary muscles controlled by the same organ.

Xibalbá :: Weary

Light tires you. Whiteness a trap. Galaxies orbit areolas.

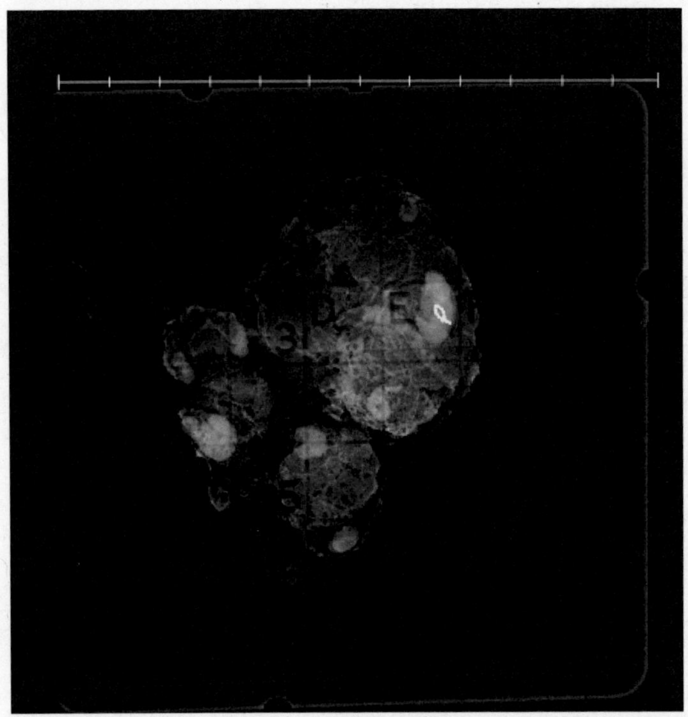

Silent feed.

On Unknowing

Taxol causes neuropathy. ~~It's one thing to be told something exists, another to feel that something existing. I think about desire next to experience. I think of force next to experience. All the words we string together, always unable. In late January, my fingers began to throb. By February the burns & stings crawled up my forearms. By early March, a lowered dose. By mid-March, the oncologist suggested skipping an infusion. By late March, M, the PA, stood just inside the curtain of my infusion area saying,~~ *Your choice. We can't lower the dose anymore. If we stop the treatment now, you run the risk of cancer returning.* ~~Many times the neuropathy goes away.~~ *Sometimes it's permanent.* ~~Her hands slid in & out of her pockets. I notice hands now. The choices in cancer treatment continue to catch me off guard. Stop the pain or risk cancer coming back.~~ Choice guarantees nothing. ~~A fight is a fight just with choice thrown in. Four months later, I wake around 3 AM, hands searing. The website tells me damaged nerves try to repair themselves. Axons. Axons: the elongated portion of the neurons. All tendril tendril. All looking for touch. Axons shrink. Axons rest. For about a month. One day, these axons begin to regenerate. One millimeter per day. Equivalent to 1000 micrometers, or 5/127 of an inch. Just over an inch per month. I imagine my axons, feet up on the couch, slurping raspberry slushies. The website tells me the extent of recovery for nerve fibers varies. Regardless of recovery,~~ the nerve fibers will always be incomplete. ~~My phone screen lights up my face in the dark. I think about~~ incompleteness. ~~How I turn to my body as the place to contemplate gaps, as gap. How removal or what goes missing comprises only portions of incomplete. I think how treatment feels like asking to~~ kill my nerves so cancer doesn't kill me. Something horrid murmurs in the unknowing. ~~Choices feeling like zero-sum games. Then I close my eyes. I imagine the slushy-sucking axons on the couch, wondering what's worth the fight.~~ *Dear nerve fibers,* ~~I get it. I chose to damage you. Behind eyelids, I see forms nestled between soma & terminals, expand.~~ *Let us grow. If unable*~~, I still believe in you.~~ Something lovely murmurs in the unknowing. ~~Axon after axon gathers energy, stretches, seedling-esque—even then, what guarantee beyond belief—beyond nuclei.~~

All the Layers of a World Inside Me :: Ode to the Ceiba Tree :: Where Itzam-Yeh Perches

After Chichén Itzá, after the Schele drawings of Itzam-Yeh

You grow, Ya'ache', *World Tree* :: how the peccary,
pig-hoofed in their mammalian desires, long
to gouge at your sides rip pieces from your trunk ::

so you grow with spikes :: understanding
what makes you dangerous keeps you
alive :: I too grew with thorns

breaching flesh :: when dissolving occurs—
call this *maturation* for the fallible sake
of naming—traces exist on undersides

of epidermis :: your spikes disappear
what damage done in defending oneself
since birth :: my throat full of knives :: I

turn the sharp parts of me internal :: I
bruise tender muscles in each swallow :: You
bolster while I still slicing my own organs

raw :: once I held the universe

in my spine, rocked the gods in slumber
in each clavicle :: I long
for the cosmos in your stature :: to be

born, celestial :: roots tickle bellies

of demons while kapok—silky
in your pochote—mingles with gods :: life

in three realms :: *Middle World* :: your trunk
sprouts from crocodile's back :: nine
layers of *Underworld*, an inverse pyramid :: each

tendril of you burrows into a belt :: each belt
one of the nine Lords of Night :: 13 deities, each
inhabit their own layer of *Upperworld* :: In highest

branch, Itzam-Yeh proclaims, *Look, I am*
brighter than the sun :: *Nest of all nests* :: in your arms
he injects life forces, entwines cords :: You, Serpent

Bird, Seven-Macaw, laughing falcon—form makes

no difference :: My *form* :: I *do* :: What am I
in my doing :: What is my *doing* :: *My doing* :: *My*
doing :: all my wounds nestle between folds

of brain :: Does Itzam-Yeh believe my body
worthy of godly walkways :: When his nest lights up
Earth's face, does my face illuminate as pinprick

of pinpricks :: I grow out of myself :: less
Itzam-Yeh's dwelling, more all layers
of world inside me :: a whole world :: before

carcass :: my own Ceiba tree :: in a universe
of 7.75 billion Ceiba trees :: name this forest :: name
this *sacred* :: before language's inadequate husk ::

Undulations :: Plate 26

{Death's Head :: Center Direction}

Directions exist in the underworld. Where we all wound, circular, compass licked by the nails of gods & spun & spun. Mixcóatl, god of the hunt, patron of the South lives at top—what a page might possibly capture in all this spinning—for the jaws of the God of Death open. The feeling of being hunted slides between each vertebra & center lives here, inside a skull, inside the turntable of inevitable, in this quiet pause in the land of no-living.

Fallacy of pause.
Fallacy of pause.
Pause fallacy of pause.
Pause fallacy of pause fallacy.
Fallacy of fallacy of pause pause.

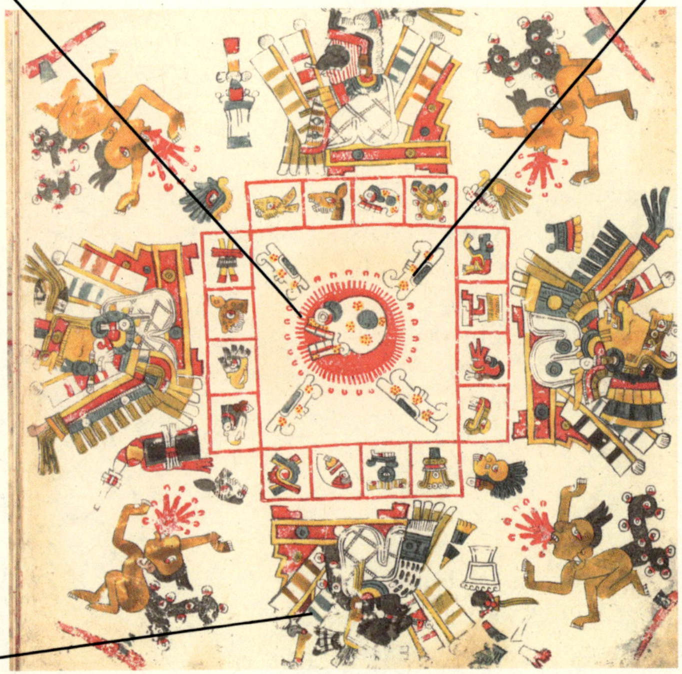

{Funerary Bundles}

{Fo(u)r Long Bones}

What we find in the appendicular skeleton: tibia, fibula, femur, metatarsals, phalanges.

What we find in the upper limbs: humerus radius, ulna, metacarpals, phalanges.

Our medullary cavity. When extremities bulge a brain. When spongy. We so spongy. *Which long bone are you?* When *one of fo(u)r* responds.

When positioned under flesh. When removed. When fo(u)r long bones circle. When *where lies the rest of us*. When fo(u)r long bones point to & away. When summoned. When fo(u)r longbones find their way outside the body. When fo(u)r long bones stretch, mid jumping jack. When giddy. When play play. When fo(u)r long bones mimic limbs for a skull; the God of Death's skull. When fo(u)r long bones, *You have my attention. Show me how you preform.*

If I sleep. If weight of stillness from once not still. Let me find gods escaping from my pores. Let me find gods wrapping their tongues around my wrists, threading me through soil to cloud to become comet's nucleus, comet's anatomy: the leftovers. Let me be the leftovers: interplanetary dust particles: bits of graphite, bits of diamond, bits of titanium cloistered inside frozen gases of H_2O, CO_2, NH_3, HCN that form the barrier between magnetic & cometopause. Feel my pull. Closer I get to the sun, I spew gases & dust into a glowing head. I glow. Glow with me. I glow. Glow as in *I too know how to burn.*

Xibalba :: Wilt

In the shop window, your hair turtles out from follicles. You crack open the word *beautiful* & a mouth full of ants scatter to the ground. Thoraxes writhing. Tongue-esque.

*

You examine the heap. The syllables & letters, a typography of bodies squirming to puzzle the mess. How to translate your body to the world. The left implant inches under skin, rashes, as if to answer the answerless. You itch. Feel curls of your flesh under your nailbeds.

*

At 45, you cancer ridden. You cut open. You *survive survive* they say. The *theys* tire you.

*

In an apartment in Portland, you watch the movie *Flashdance*. Fixate on the montage of firm, thin thighs running in place. *Headless*. World making women headless thighs. You later learn a professional choreographer took Jennifer Beals' place in all dance scenes. How each carefully constructed head tilt & wig placement designed to not give away the body double.

Who plays you after the fade? Who doubles for you?

*

To long for youth seems deceptively easy & inextricably inaccurate. Your body in-progress, a maturation of soft tissues & synapses, desires acknowledgement. You do not long for youth. You love the wilt. Messy wilt. No, you long for articulation. Articulation in a language obsessed with *not-your-body*. Obsessed with illusions.

*

How often you fall. Seismic into the unseen as unseen. Invisibility: a power of goddesses. You, god-mess. Tricky god-mess. Speaking you into form.

Inhabit Plurally

a gap forms in your mandibles—casket refusing to shut :: gap only a wound, if un-mended ::

Trace anything long enough you feel the grooves, the imprints the *who* of *who came before* ::
interest in the after :: as in *here I am* :: *the one who spends her time wading in the after* ::
you came to see what you've never known

only felt :: :: an empty that sometimes screams :: beneath eyelids ::
how gaps sometimes mean erasure. :: sometimes ::

love for the gap ::

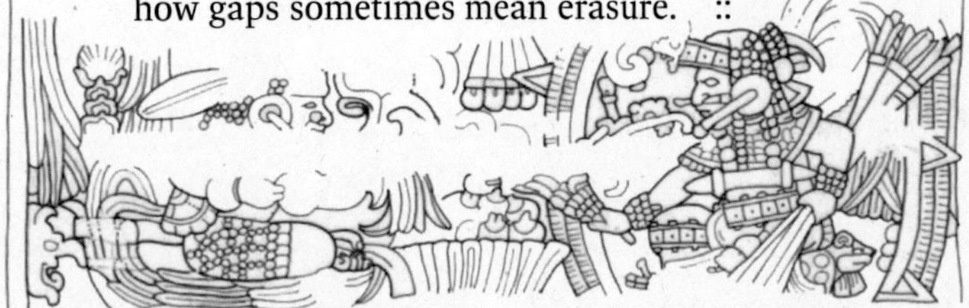

fleshy symbol ::

:: please let there be love :: :: or { } continues to define ::

The Great Ball Court structure almost rubble— importance of *almost* :: an influx—a pulse
through time {a star collapsing in your gut} :: the word *ancestor* nettles down your spine :: to inhabit, plurally
some fragments lead to stitching :: some fragments rebuild
our bones :: across a border we want to call *space-time continuum* :: you feel the rip of fabric {a tear of bandage
ready for application} :: you welcome your body to a thin & frail passage :: a homecoming ::

of after :: after Linda left Francisco, after the bruise, the blood, after the punched solar plexus, after the *you dirty beaners*, after
the *Why don't you just go back to Mexico's* after the food bank steps, after K**** forcing you to shave our legs at seven because
your black hair was *disgusting* to her blonde, after your own grandfather called you *filth*, *worthless*, after after after after

:: *after* of thought rippling time :: *after* of Spanish left your body hollow :: You understand ache

More Eyes Toward Detection

we have to learn to turn toward

Sara Ahmed, *Living a Feminist Life*

Enoughness (n.) (v.)

e.nough.ness (uh-NUFF-nuhss)

1. : I am
    1. (See:

I am I am I am I am I am I am I am I am I am I am I am I am

nough Enough Enough Enough Enough Enough Enough Enough Enough Enough Enough Enough Enough Enough Enough Enough Enough Enough Enough Enou

Bell ringing. March 27, 2023. After five months of chemotherapy.

Bell ringing. July 10, 2023. After twenty-five days of radiation.

IamIamIamIamIamIamIamIamIamIamIamIamI

Undulations :: Plate 22

{Pierce/Leak}

Stagnancy. How a sharp thing remains motionless until *action*. All about action. Then slash/slash/slash. Brutality of words. How language holds us so delicately tendoned— until slash/slash /slash. Not even *until*. Often the slash & slay serpentine inside the hold. How we coil/uncoil. Male deer with an arrow through a rib. See your dick red, tongue red, knuckles red, eye red, gums red. Someone stabbed you, head turned, vision to horizon of conifer, cloud forest, alpine grassland. Briefly, you believed in celestial space, believed in hums chorusing your chest. What heavens knew you. What you saw before pierce: speculation. What leaks? What do any of us see before slash/slash/slash. What leaks? Born to be pierced. Born to pierce.

{Aftershocks}

My research tells me: left deer caught in acts of impalement; right deer dead. I reject death of the right deer. I know the deer is dead, research says so. Yet, I reject dying. Impermanently. Momentarily. I reject dying to remain in the realm of possibility. Such as: 800 years ago, in the highlands of what-was-not-known-as Mexico, artists painted two deer & one half of the Tōnalpōhualli on animal skin. While they painted, they thought of me. Not specifically, *Damn, can't wait for ______ to see & completely fuck up by misinterpreting,* but more generally, *Remember us.* & I hear *Remember us* in the shower. *Remember us* while pulling weeds. *Remember us* when walking my Great Pyrenees. *Remember us* in bread. *Remember us* in mammograms of my remaining breast. *Remember us* as tinnitus, a low tone keeping my brain company in the void. & I feel remembered. & *us* becomes *we*, so, yes, Death, I reject you. Corti utter & utter.

{A Pseudo-Prayer for Echoes in Lungs & Stars}

Anatomy: a chilly word. Word with a type of formality, sciencey. A lifeless word about *life* brought *to* life by use in the mouth. Am I not (semi)defined by my cognition's use of all these muscles gathering? Gathering *to*? The *to* being the meat here. Literal meat-puppet & also figurative leap. *To to to to to to to to to to to.* So much of us lingers on the precipice before & after *to*. I want to believe all the anatomical in me (as me) might heal itself. I dig into the guts of me: hollowed organs, twisting tubes, intestines, leaf-shaped pancreas tucked under the liver—gentle lovers. I dig into the tissues of organs, into the intercellular matrix; wrap my brain in wet webbing; dig until I scrape the universe edges; scratch, tab-like, with my nail to uncover Deep Time & everything witchy & pulsating inside me from the first formless, shapeless void (voidness so holy, so present), leans in to say__________ , to _________ .

Xibalbá :: Holes

Kukulcán manifested as Quetzalcóatl to the Toltecs & Aztecs. Feather serpent god. Creator god. Bringer of rains. Bringer of wind. Rain pummels the Temple of Kukulcán, pummels my body. I feel Kukulcán in the squish between my toes. Bringer of soaking hair. Bringer of the sky's wail.

*

I count the nine tiers of the temple. The ancient Maya believed the underworld consisted of nine layers ruled by nine gods. Or twelve. Or fourteen. Holes pock ancient Mesoamerican history.

Being full of holes myself, this connection comforts me.

*

The *Popol Vuh* says to reach the nineth level, the dead must traverse jagged mountains, knives, scorpion-infested rivers, & ripping out one's heart to give as sacrifice.

What do I rip my heart out for?

*

The rain descends harder. *Bringer of rains*. The tour moves on from Kukulcán's temple. *What might my godly power entail*?

Bringer of hugs. Bringer of therapist-after-therapist-after-therapist. Bringer of double-jointed thumbs. Bringer of no-broken-bones-but-plenty-of-barbed-wire-scars. Bringer of believing the naturalness of density. Bringer of removals—all the -ectomies & the vestiges of evolving made known through ache. Bringer of smiles-so-wide-eyes-become-slits. Bringer of fatherless ________. Bringer of British-mystery marathons. Bringer of ~~shame in~~ my Spanish~~-less~~(building) tongue. Bringer of bare feet in mulberry trees. Bringer of ghosts (who-play-tricks-&-follow-you-from-house-to-house -but-never-scare-you). Bringer of poems where I contemplate being a *bringer of*. Bringer of believing Garza's "sometimes a rectangle is a sacred shape." Bringer of smelling-inside-every-book. Bringer of orgasms. Bringer of ~~what-stalks-me-in-my-own-breast-tissues~~ (what remains).

*

Bringer of holes. Lovely holes. Holes
so round, so robust, they couldn't possibly be flaws,
couldn't possibly be wounds.

*

Holes on the inside & outside of flesh—

where I fall backward into myself, fall through galaxy's fabric, through spacetime, the multiverse, to find Xibalbá full of:

god-&-dead-soul dance-parties; the pups who died of bone cancer & lymphoma leaping & playing; lilies & carnations—miles & miles of carnations; banned books, burned books; tea-parties inside turtle carapaces; carapaces the size of sky scrapers; the ozone clean & clear & all the mouths gulping as if breathing meant tasting the heavens; the cassette tape of Grandma Evelyn talking about the Maypole Festival in Germany; all extinct biodiversity alive gorging surface after surface & crevasse after crevasse; the one photo of Jose Francisco Zamora that I hid & hated & long for now; bicycles—every single god & human soul peddling & ringing bells & dressed in costume—parade after parade of bicycles.

*

I close my eyes. I see Kukulcán's feathers flapping veil-esque on a ten-speed.

My feathers flapping in the wind. The wind
I create with each turn of each pedal.

Ecogodliness

Our story of the world. Our. Our. Our. Do our jaws get numb
from gulping our *ours* over & over—guppies in our freshwater aquariums?

Christensen wonders where art necessitates. Are we only forces of nature's
workplace? The naturalness in my muscles, cells, saliva knows conjurings, knows

fallacies. Are we our own workplace? I peck my ovaling mouth at the air. I wonder
about myopic gestures. How I desire to be special. Yet change & chance. How I desire

to be special. Yet I've felt the punch of *order*, the kick of someone else's specialness
over mine, hot breath & eyes cutting me up. Being no paper doll. We mistake

something sharp for believable, a well-manicured thing as authority. Being paper
more than once, I wish to resist cutting another. Our. Our. Our. I wonder who the *our*

of *our story* really means. I wonder about extinction. I kneel down in the bee balm. Smell
the bergamot orange. Dream of the blue corporal dragonfly—how the endangered

soak up their days. Dream of tubercled blossom, pearly mussel, extinct in the state
I live. How do we know we are on the precipice? Downy woodpecker acrobatically forages,

drums in woodlots, quietly digs & feeds in bark. Downy woodpecker flocks to the feeder
of black oil sunflowers & millet. When the feeder empties, when all the feeders empty,

the downy woodpecker moves on, departs. Never thinks once, *Where have they gone?*

Message to the Young Goddess of the Moon

No thoughts to say about the moon. The novelist jokes about not being a poet. I feel the lie. Every person once immature, once glowing. I begin to ask, ~~*What place for me in luminary reflections?*~~ I know the question to be inadequate. You know the sensuous. You know vegetation. *Precious feather flower*. Human knowing: incoherent whispers, aches in shins, tingling sclera—what exists beyond vision. Inability to fathom. Unableness: a gift. Elliptical parts of me. Xochiquétzal, lunar disc in your chest, I am the heart cradled in your ribs. I sprout—becoming the multivalenced tree you dream of me.

Xibalbá :: Extinction

Eighteen species of fireflies face extinction. I hold a boxed-in flutter beneath my sternum. *Vanishing,* the *National Geographic* article warns. Then on: about creating a habitat in my backyard & on: about turning outside lights off at night & on: about ditching pesticides & on. My brain still stuck on the word *extinction*. My brain still stuck on little-me's brain spinning in my skull outside the motel, first week in June, barefoot, eyelids all a blink blink blink as bulbed-abdomens wink-flash in the dark. Stars in the mulberries. Stars in the pasture. Flitter of small limbs in an earthly universe. How larvae live underground during winter, mature in spring & emerge burning in summer. All that dwells under worlds as worlds. How all winter long *hidden* means *incubation*. My empty glass jars—my inability to place a lid on anything that might burst wings & fly. My empty glass jars. How down the hill kids forgot to pock holes in metal before scooping in the small bodies. My empty glass jars. How any excess light hinders the mating rituals of fluttering bioluminescence. Ancient Maya believed the Milky Way to be the road to Xibalbá. What glitters. What seduces. Empty glass jars. How clipping wings equates to a type of death. After the four stages of metamorphosis: eggs, larvae, pupae, & adult, an adult firefly no longer molts. Limb-wings. Empty jars. The *empty* of empty. E-words burrow again. All the species' names to place beside *ex- ex- ex- ex-*. Litany of ex-. Another spinning in my adult brain. I exfoliate my scapulas—to prime, to soften possible surfaces—for breach.

Archive Notes #5 :: Codex Yoalli Ehēcatl, Vatican Apostolic Library, September 2022

one (dot dot :   death's
evidence   . Why deviate
all   this
thinking?
I move   I see   the body   arches
convexes   feels sacred
with   touch   sense
the many angles
What   I search   for
about me   brought me here   this document

wrinkles   flesh toward the

missing
. Do we
disintegrate   ? Do we dig

the edges
physically, with ancestors
I feel   beyond
understanding
to know
the unnamed who once had names. I   stand
present
,   drawn to

feel akin to
this moment.   look   my
skin

not removed from my ancestors
I am here with them. I is enough I
feel enough.
love jumps off the page
seems surreal.
I lower wings

to the spirits. I use

tongue to
wonder
bodily in
worship

Xibalbá :: Shape

Starlings know to veer. Anatomically attuned to each premonition of each starling. Sacred space.

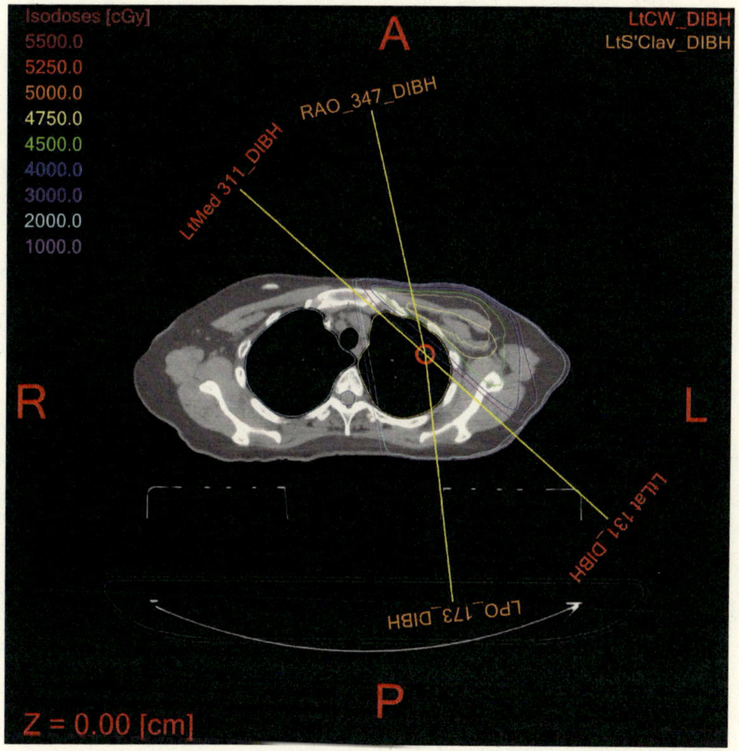

Shared prayer. Air: collective figuration. Wormholes folding. The unimaginable. Ever so brief. I, too,

an undulation. I see the shape before the shape. Feel the constellation forming in my spine.

Summoning Huixtocihuatl at My Annual Physical: Two Months Before Diagnosis

Do you eat enough salt? Dr. S. raises eyes
over my knobby knees
my dark nipples under the gown—

deep in scribbles, I imagine
her clipboard full of brazen loops
& typography anatomy goddesses

& orthographers might praise
in ritual sacrifice. What Dr. S. doesn't know:
I lust for sodium chloride. I wake

in the night with .4% of my body
weight shimmying like that Dancing Bird
of Paradise opening his mating ritual

with a bow. Spinning plume twirls—my body
courting any conduit to douse
in salt. Salt on my eggs [a given,

you say], raw kohlrabi, in boiling
water, on my pizza, cucumbers, potatoes,
tomatoes [insert vegetable here _____],

hot dogs [yes, I eat hot dogs;
don't shame me], on ice cream [salted caramel,
duh, but really all], tacos, pasta, Tom Kha soup,

sushi, in my beer [& some
on the napkin], on burgers, in my wine,
in my bare palm [sprinkle sprinkle lick]. I pray

to Huixtocihuatl, *Whose sacrifice am I?* Talons
of my eagle-claw headpiece
dipped in glass shakers. *Whose 40 teaspoons am I?*

She hates how science stole her ethos, her
remedies. Her response remains ____________
& also ________; her silence echoing

as Nahuatl dormant in me. I want
to learn my body in context
of my ancestors. I am no victim.

I am a maker of salt
carrying my chords of flowers,
head adorned with garland. *I eat*

a lot of salt, I tell Dr. S.
More scribbles.
Another Dr. S. on the Well

+ Good website says I crave salt
due to habit, a high sodium
diet. I train the goddess into me. Ingestion

due to stress, excess sweating, poor
sleep. Bloodwork later shows
an iron deficiency connected to

my inoperative thyroid. Something always
laid bare on the altar
of death—one must collapse

into a broken thing
to get to the bottom of most curiosities,
most cures, to tamp down

most cravings. A goddess
if well cultivated, well conjured,
exists for this too.

{Inverted in the Dark}

How night reaches out here—the Tōnalpōhualli arranged: five rows, 20-day signs. The inverted human, not god, yet among gods. Legs separated, mid handstand, mid cartwheel, three eyes in juggle between your feet. I understand being watched; I understand moving my body to appease the eyes of others—though regret riddles the webs of me; I understand wet, licking eyes upon me in spaces where I am told *You are not brown enough* & spaces where *What are you?* prevail. I dig & dig & become an archaeologist of *enough*. Enough—monster's eyes as my eyes. Enough—of this performance. Who am I dazzling if not my own acheful wound? Enough—disbelief. Ancestors remind me how enough builds & roils in the collective. How far back must I dig to believe I am part of any collective? I turn to this Codex & find various faces of me among the rituals, various desires in meanings, lack of meanings, in how the Earth, too, contains an eye that simultaneously loves me & wants to swallow me whole. To traverse being *enough* for a god, for any god, the me-me god. & the godlessness of my belief may just be enough. Here I go again thinking of godliness inside me. I obsess over value. How *enough* has always been here, waiting for me.

{Six Feet, One Almost in Death's Jaws}

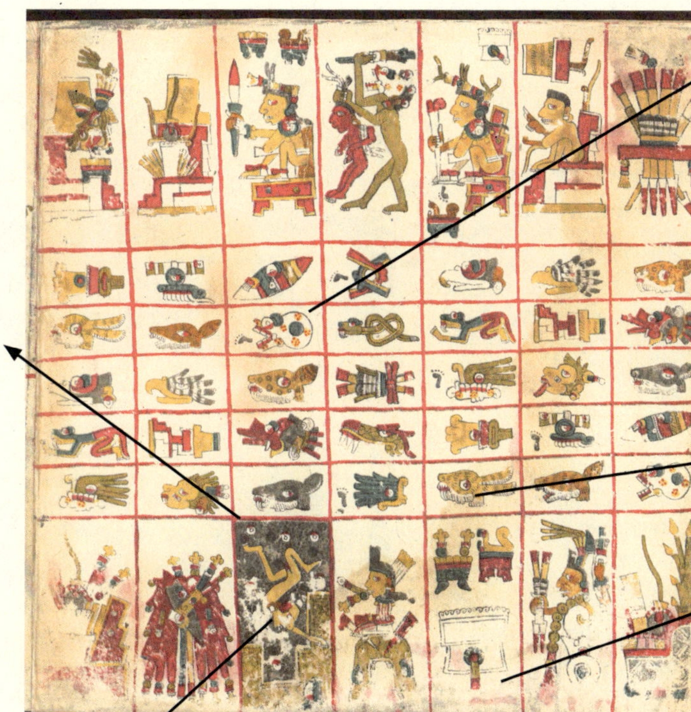

Yes, I remember you. On my heels. Let us meet in the fields. I call these fields *future*. You call these fields *timpani rising inside you*.

{Stains}

Damage; mushroom clouds across the surface; smoke damage; fire; to survive being lit aflame; *who* & *what* wants to burn you cannot fathom your body alive; to be held under water; to be sodden & thrash to leak & still remain; to survive water knowing *destruction* as the intent; to survive; how skin bears remnants, murmurs from open pores.

{Eyes Worn Off}

Time, travel & mistreatment rub any skin raw. Eyes wiped from the human. Two of the three eyes below the chin, gone. Even the Earth's eye barely visible. How we all smudge from vision one day. Whose vision? What remains after attempts of erasure: a new divination coils.

On Divination

I am attempting my own/ myth-making.

– Solmaz Sharif, *LOOK*

Your head line breaks. Vanishes.
She sits back, releasing my palms.
I want to tell her the palmar flexion creases
develop before birth. My lines form inside
the lines of my mother. How we
imprint from imprints. I want
to tell her I believe in the astral plane, twice
my brother & I talk of this plane—a place
similar to the Alden Motel: full
of energies & the dust of disbelief.

I want to tell her I believe in reincarnation
65% of the time. How I know
I'll return, *But this is my first go round*
on Earth, I tell my friends
how the cormorant's black wing tips
touching V in the field of dandelions
resembles a ceremony
of forgotten. I, too, am phantasm
to some unsuspecting future wanderer.
Who am I a ceremony of forgotten for?

I want to tell her I lie
down under lilac bushes to dream
another me out of language—of cells
& neurons firing to thought. My own
augur, I prognosticate with words
as if any story ever saves
an inner voice from an outer
destiny. I place my gaze
into the palimpsest's, *I understand*
fragmentation is a gift.

Xibalbá :: Unmyth

Fire-toothed. Smoke lungs. Raised in the belly of. Sepulcher. Dead-tread cranium. Fog so dense. What won't w[h]it[e]ness consume. Gulp. Dilation. Gulp. Lips-apart, fog-lip. Seethe. Sooth in each spark[le]. Each buoyant blaze.

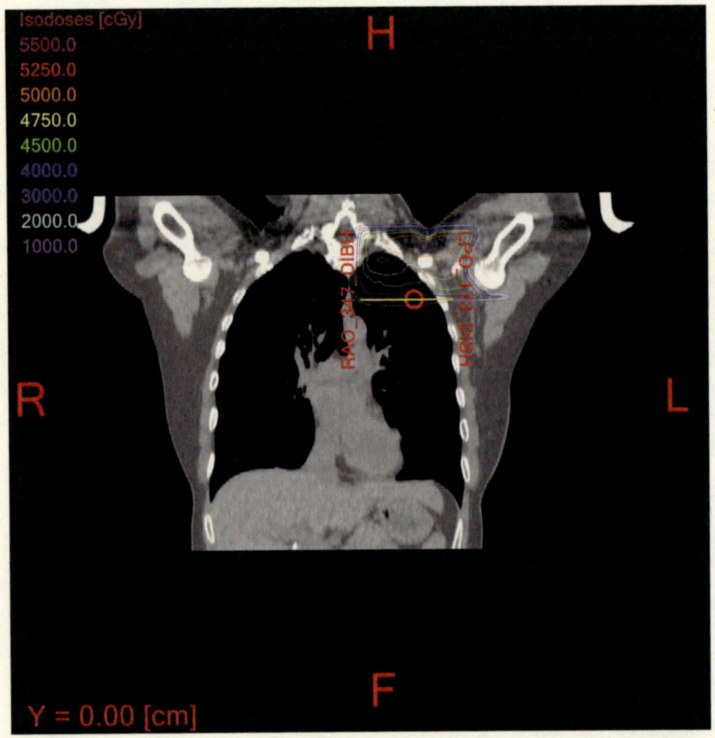

Ecogodliness

A large solar flare reaches the Earth. Geomagnetic storms make the aurora borealis visible in the Ohio sky. *Rare*. News channels report the phenomenon's appearances in October 2021 & Summer 2022. *Not so rare*. You scold your reaction & compound rarity. How two nights before, a tissue expander took space between muscle & chest lining. Today, an implant. Impermanence of clouds, clouds at night. What only appears invisible due to limitations of light or vision. What obscures. How one in eight US women develop invasive breast cancer. How you toggle back & forth in the use of the numbers 1 & 8 versus the words. Neither makes you less statistical, less science-strewn. You obsess over limits. What obscures. Emptiness of rarity when *one* encapsulates you. *One* always encapsulates you—the metaphysical, cognitive—now, though, rarity shaken & shredded. Now your naturalness unlaces, *rare*. You step barefoot onto cool grass, allowing twilight to gulp your chin, gulp your ribs, gulp your shadow—until all outlines of you hush, until cloud osmosed, nebulous.

Xibalbá :: Rebirth

Two months after your last radiation session, ocean water fills your ears. Muffle of seagull chatter. Muffle of ship horns in the distance. Muffle of the man singing to his lover in Spanish as they spoon chest-deep in waves—the very ocean gathers close to your eardrums, whispering to you in swells, beats & illegible echoes. Your body held as tender bloat, into tide.

*

You, an illegible echo pounding into nothingness. You with belief someone, something, someplace not only hears your pulses but utters back, *Hey hey, I get you.*

The whole damn world quieted.

*

The unknown quivers around you, in you—your face above the lapping into sun. Sun, Hunahpú's gift, turns the inside of your eyelids red. In suspension, the *Popol Vuh*, Hunahpú & Xbalanqué creep in. After they jumped into flames, the soothsayers spread their ashes in the Xibalbán river. The brothers transformed to fishmen. Later gods, again. Dressed as peddling performers, they returned to One Death & Seven Death trickier. You think of tricks. The flight attendant en route to the ocean stating, *We need 20 people from the front to move to the back*—only 70 people on a 175-seat 737. You wonder about ratios & weight & how comfort arrives disguised as unbalance. Did Hunahpú & Xbalanqué feel askew in their new forms—now being reborn in the waters of Xibalbá?

*

The news warns of dangerous rip tides. A new hurricane forming in the Pacific. Illegibility a type of rip tide promising then withholding. You always wonder: *Illegible to whom*?

*

Cells inside you wonder why you wonder so much.

*

Coastlines. Where any body meets another body. All crash crash crash. All anticipation. All flooding forward. All tearing back. Desire in the repeat. Desire in the repeat.

*

You flip your body from float to stand. To your left, a moon jellyfish—clear & mushroom-headed with red gonads visible announces to you, *Hey, hey, I am here too. Aloneness, nah. Just float.* You see Xbalanqué cutting off Hunahpú's head. Growing it back. You hear One Death & Seven Death screeching, *Now me! My turn!*

How many tricks does it take?

The inevitability of the Lords of Xibalbá losing heads. Inevitability of the Hero Twins winning. Inevitability of any story ending in *clap clap.* In any story ending: ends string from. A story. A moral. A story. A mortal. Did Xbalanqué & Hunahpú's risk as gods tricking?

*

Remember Y's words, *Mortality makes people squirmy.* Your own trickiness. You & moon jellyfish, side-by-side. Briefly squirmless. Briefly aware. Before the tide moves you both, into a wayward muffle.

On Blessings & Want

A Cumulus cloud streaks the belly of horizon, reminds me of the illusion of stillness; both inside & outside the flesh. How I used to long to be still—now, I am learning to long to understand the lack of stillness.

*

A bee doesn't think of its buzz; nor does a bee flap its wings. Only nectar & hover & pollination & honey & hive. Innate buzz cradled intricately inside flight muscles pulling on a springy thorax wall, in & out, to create a *pingpingping* sound.

*

A bee's muscles contract multiple times from a single nerve impulse & combined actions make the bee beat each wing—each wing in cycle 230 times per second. Each minute a 13,800 wing-beat blessing. Each buzz brought by Wind to an ear canal, another blessing.

I search for blessings now.

*

I find myself flapping; anatomically & cognitively going nowhere; I still cannot comprehend some of my own patterns; how beating in my organs not only doesn't cease, but sometimes I feel wounds from my own imaginary fists punching behind my ribcage, behind my ocular bones.

*

I want to heal.

I want to heal in a world where carbon emissions don't eat the world first; where greenhouse gases stop trapping heat; where the pumpkins rotting in the dump don't turn to methane; all the methane building & those ghostly fists pummel & pummel; where I don't worry about what clouds bring first, before worrying about the clouds themselves.

*

A wickedness to want wanting.

*

So I learn from the clouds. Look for blessings before each frost. Blessings within each crystalline formation. I open to stillnessless in all my biological humming. Bless my openings, my permeable epidermis.

Bless my surfaces seen & unseen.

Bless my jaw in boney hingeness. Bless my mutation of mutability, cloud-esque. Bless all my Stratocumulus all Nimbostratus all Cirrocumulus—let me paint the sky.

Bless the air that moves through me.

*

Bless the bees. O please let the bees become un-endangered.

Bless floating water.

*

In all my formations, I bow to Mother Wind, in her gentle embrace, terrible embrace. Behind my breastbone a *thud, thud.* Bless me Mother, I am your hapless daughter. I forget you, then falls to my knees, myocardium gasping, *Shape me.*

In Communion With

"Now it still ripples, now it still murmurs, ripples, it still sighs, still hums, and it is empty under sky." Unknown, *Popol Vuh*. Translated by Dennis Tedlock. *Popol Vuh: The Mayan Book of the Dawn of Life*, pg. 6. A Touchstone Book, Simon & Schuster, 1996.

"These places will leak their histories and will void; they will burn lines into the walls of the page and will haunt the periphery with figuration." Renee Gladman, "FIG. 55," *Plans for Sentences*, pg. 111. Wave Books, 2022.

In "Undulation (n.) (v.)" the mention of Vicuña is Cecilia Vicuña and her book *Instan.*

"Undulation (n.) (v.)," contains the quote, "A movement comes into existence to transform what is in existence," Sara Ahmed, "Introduction: *Bringing Feminist Theory Home*," *Living a Feminist Life*, pg. 3. Duke University Press, 2017.

The word "Ollin" means *movement* and is one of the 20-day signs from the Tōnalpōhualli in the Codex Yoalli Ehēcatl.

All "Undulations" poem sequence were written after an archival visit to the Vatican Apostolic Library in Vatican City where I was allowed to spend two days with the Codex Yoalli Ehēcatl. During this visit, I studied the Codex, turned the pages, and was immersed with the physical text. The Codex is an accordion-style document read from right to left, and often serpentine. The "Undulations" sequence displayed in this book is in reverse beginning with Plate 73 (even though there are 76 plates in the Codex). This reversal compliments the complexity of my own lacks (language and culture) along with the large gaps in lineage forced upon decedents of ancient Mesoamerica. This book does not seek exactness.

The "Inceptions/Undulations" page that begins the book, as well as the "Undulations" sequence, are influenced by information in the following source texts.

> *The Codex Borgia: A Full-Color Restoration of the Ancient Mexican Manuscript* by Gisele Díaz & Alan Rogers with commentary by Bruce E. Byland, Dover Publications, 1993.
>
> The Ancient America's website at the Los Angeles County Museum of Art (LACMA, http://ancientamericas.org/).
>
> "Aztec manuscript under the microscope," by Vahé Ter Minassian in *The Guardian*, November 28, 2014.

"Tōnalpōhualli The Human Relationship with Time & Space," with Dr. Alex Mazatl Ojeda YouTube, uploaded by Ehēcatl Wind Philosophies, September 16, 2021.

Permission granted by the Los Angeles County Museum of Art (LACMA) Ancient Americas to use the high-resolution images of Codex Yoalli Ehēcatl (Codex Borgia) in these poems, as well as all the Mesoamerican drawings from Chichén Itzá by Linda Schele, David Schele, and Mark van Stone. Poems with these images and drawings include the following in order they appear in the book:

"Undulations :: Plate 73" - Codex Yoalli Ehēcatl (Codex Borgia), Loubat Edition 1898, Page/Plate: 73, Courtesy Ancient Americas at LACMA (ancientamericas.org), in conjunction with Universitätsbibliothek Rostock, Bibliothek der Berlin-Brandenburgischen Akademie der Wissenschaften (BBAW) and Staats- und Universitätsbibliothek Hamburg, with thanks to Michael Dürr FAMSI project coordinator, Mr. Rosenau of Mikro-Univers, Ms. Danielewski and Dr. Thiemer-Sachse of the Free University of Berlin.

"Xibalbá :: How One Body Carries" – "SD-5051" Drawing Chichen Itza Maya. Drawing by Mark van Stone © David Schele Photo courtesy Ancient Americas at LACMA (ancientamericas.org)

"Undulations :: Plate 71" - Codex Yoalli Ehēcatl (Codex Borgia), Loubat Edition 1898, Page/Plate: 71, Courtesy Ancient Americas at LACMA (ancientamericas.org), in conjunction with Universitätsbibliothek Rostock, Bibliothek der Berlin-Brandenburgischen Akademie der Wissenschaften (BBAW) and Staats- und Universitätsbibliothek Hamburg, with thanks to Michael Dürr FAMSI project coordinator, Mr. Rosenau of Mikro-Univers, Ms. Danielewski and Dr. Thiemer-Sachse of the Free University of Berlin.

"Message to Rabbit in the Moon" – Image taken from, Codex Yoalli Ehēcatl (Codex Borgia), Loubat Edition 1898, Page/Plate: 71, Courtesy Ancient Americas at LACMA (ancientamericas.org), in conjunction with Universitätsbibliothek Rostock, Bibliothek der Berlin-Brandenburgischen Akademie der Wissenschaften (BBAW) and Staats- und Universitätsbibliothek Hamburg, with thanks to Michael Dürr FAMSI project coordinator, Mr. Rosenau of Mikro-Univers, Ms. Danielewski and Dr. Thiemer-Sachse of the Free University of Berlin.

"Undulations :: Plate 53" - Codex Yoalli Ehēcatl (Codex Borgia), Loubat Edition 1898, Page/Plate 53, Courtesy Ancient Americas at LACMA (ancientamericas.org), in conjunction with Universitätsbibliothek Rostock, Bibliothek der Berlin-Brandenburgischen Akademie der Wissenschaften (BBAW) and Staats- und Universitätsbibliothek Hamburg, with thanks to Michael Dürr FAMSI project coordinator, Mr. Rosenau of Mikro-Univers, Ms. Danielewski and Dr. Thiemer-Sachse of the Free University of Berlin.

"Vision Offerings" – "SD-5026," Chichén Itzá Maya. Drawing by Linda Schele © David Schele Photo courtesy Ancient Americas at LACMA (ancientamericas.org).

"Undulations :: Plate 44" - Codex Yoalli Ehēcatl (Codex Borgia), Loubat Edition 1898, Page/Plate: 44, Courtesy Ancient Americas at LACMA (ancientamericas.org), in conjunction with Universitätsbibliothek Rostock, Bibliothek der Berlin-Brandenburgischen Akademie der Wissenschaften (BBAW) and Staats- und Universitätsbibliothek Hamburg, with thanks to Michael Dürr FAMSI project coordinator, Mr. Rosenau of Mikro-Univers, Ms. Danielewski and Dr. Thiemer-Sachse of the Free University of Berlin.

"Xibalbá :: Desire" - "SD-5068" Chichén Itzá Maya. Drawing by Linda Schele © David Schele. Photo courtesy Ancient Americas at LACMA (ancientamericas.org)

"Message to the Skeletal Earth Goddess" image taken from, Codex Yoalli Ehēcatl (Codex Borgia), Loubat Edition 1898, Page/Plate 44, Courtesy Ancient Americas at LACMA (ancientamericas.org), in conjunction with Universitätsbibliothek Rostock, Bibliothek der Berlin-Brandenburgischen Akademie der Wissenschaften (BBAW) and Staats- und Universitätsbibliothek Hamburg, with thanks to Michael Dürr FAMSI project coordinator, Mr. Rosenau of Mikro-Univers, Ms. Danielewski and Dr. Thiemer-Sachse of the Free University of Berlin.

"Undulations :: Plate 39" - Codex Yoalli Ehēcatl (Codex Borgia), Loubat Edition 1898, Page/Plate: 39, Courtesy Ancient Americas at LACMA (ancientamericas.org), in conjunction with Universitätsbibliothek Rostock, Bibliothek der Berlin-Brandenburgischen Akademie der Wissenschaften (BBAW) and Staats- und Universitätsbibliothek Hamburg, with thanks to Michael Dürr FAMSI project coordinator, Mr. Rosenau of Mikro-Univers, Ms. Danielewski and Dr. Thiemer-Sachse of the Free University of Berlin.

"Plaything" - Codex Yoalli Ehēcatl (Codex Borgia), Loubat Edition 1898, Page/Plate: 2 & 71, Courtesy Ancient Americas at LACMA (ancientamericas.org), in conjunction with Universitätsbibliothek Rostock, Bibliothek der Berlin-Brandenburgischen Akademie der Wissenschaften (BBAW) and Staats- und Universitätsbibliothek Hamburg, with thanks to Michael Dürr FAMSI project coordinator, Mr. Rosenau of Mikro-Univers, Ms. Danielewski and Dr. Thiemer-Sachse of the Free University of Berlin.

"A Story for the Cosmos" – "SD-5052," Chichén Itzá Maya. Drawing by Mark van Stone © David Schele Photo courtesy Ancient Americas at LACMA (ancientamericas.org).

"Message to the Goddess of Running Water" image taken from, Codex Yoalli Ehēcatl (Codex Borgia), Loubat Edition 1898, Page/Plate: 53, Courtesy Ancient Americas at LACMA (ancientamericas.org), in conjunction with Universitätsbibliothek Rostock, Bibliothek der Berlin-Brandenburgischen Akademie der Wissenschaften (BBAW) and Staats- und Universitätsbibliothek Hamburg, with thanks to Michael Dürr FAMSI project coordinator, Mr. Rosenau of Mikro-Univers, Ms. Danielewski and Dr. Thiemer-Sachse of the Free University of Berlin.

"Undulations :: Plate 29" - Codex Yoalli Ehēcatl (Codex Borgia), Loubat Edition 1898, Page/Plate: 29, Courtesy Ancient Americas at LACMA (ancientamericas.org), in conjunction with Universitätsbibliothek Rostock, Bibliothek der Berlin-Brandenburgischen Akademie der Wissenschaften (BBAW) and Staats- und Universitätsbibliothek Hamburg, with thanks to Michael Dürr FAMSI project coordinator, Mr. Rosenau of Mikro-Univers, Ms. Danielewski and Dr. Thiemer-Sachse of the Free University of Berlin.

"All the Layers of the World Inside Me" - "SD-3514," Chichén Itzá Maya. Drawing by Linda Schele © David Schele Photo courtesy Ancient Americas at LACMA (ancientamericas.org).

"Inhabit Plurally" – Image of wooden lintel, inner doorway in the upper Temple of the Jaguar, Great Ballcourt. "SD-5062," Chichén Itzá Maya. Drawing by Linda Schele © David Schele Photo courtesy Ancient Americas at LACMA (ancientamericas.org).

"Undulations :: Plate 22" - Codex Yoalli Ehēcatl (Codex Borgia), Loubat Edition 1898, Page/Plate: 22, Courtesy Ancient Americas at LACMA (ancientamericas.org), in conjunction with Universitätsbibliothek Rostock, Bibliothek der Berlin-Brandenburgischen Akademie der Wissenschaften (BBAW) and Staats- und Universitätsbibliothek Hamburg, with thanks to Michael Dürr FAMSI project coordinator, Mr. Rosenau of Mikro-Univers, Ms. Danielewski and Dr. Thiemer-Sachse of the Free University of Berlin.

"Message to the Young Goddess of the Moon" image taken from, Codex Borgia, Loubat Edition 1898, Page/Plate: 44, Courtesy Ancient Americas at LACMA (ancientamericas.org), in conjunction with Universitätsbibliothek Rostock, Bibliothek der Berlin-Brandenburgischen Akademie der Wissenschaften (BBAW) and Staats- und Universitätsbibliothek Hamburg, with thanks to Michael Dürr FAMSI project coordinator, Mr. Rosenau of Mikro-Univers, Ms. Danielewski and Dr. Thiemer-Sachse of the Free University of Berlin.

"Undulations :: Plate 8" - Codex Yoalli Ehēcatl (Codex Borgia), Loubat Edition 1898, Page/Plate: 8, Courtesy Ancient Americas at LACMA (ancientamericas.org), in conjunction with Universitätsbibliothek Rostock, Bibliothek der Berlin-Brandenburgischen Akademie der Wissenschaften (BBAW) and Staats- und Universitätsbibliothek Hamburg, with thanks to Michael Dürr FAMSI project coordinator, Mr. Rosenau of Mikro-Univers, Ms. Danielewski and Dr. Thiemer-Sachse of the Free University of Berlin.

"Xibalbá :: Tunneling," uses the quote *"an infinite collection of bodyings,"* Julietta Singh's, "The Body Archive," *No Archive Will Restore You*, pg. 31. Punctum Books, 2018.

The image in the poem "[Pretending]" is a photo I took at Palatine Hill, Rome, 14 days before my mastectomy. This was a hard photo to look at. I'm in gratitude to Dr. Holli Carrell whose docupoems inspired this piece.

The poems "Archive Notes #1-5" sequence are all erasures of my notes while in the Vatican Apostolic Library from the two, three-hour blocks I spent with the Codex Yoalli Ehēcatl in September 2022. These erasures preserve the location of words and punctuation in my unrevised notes. No photography, pens, pencils, or notebooks were allowed in the Vatican Apostolic Library. Only a laptop was allowed.

"I Carry a Wor{l}d Inside Me," contains the quote "The unconscious is the most evasive archive of all, yet is pulsing right there inside you," Julietta Singh, "The Ghost Archive," No *Archive Will Restore You*, pg. 97. Punctum Books, 2018.

The images in poems, "I Carry a Wor{l}d Inside Me," "Xibalbá :: Patience," "Xibalbá :: Minuscule Devils," "Xibalbá :: Weary," "Xibalbá :: Shape," and "Xibalbá :: Unmyth," are from my own medical records from my treatment of breast cancer. These images are my personal property taken from the Tri-Health medical system.

Source materials for poems influenced by Xibablá, Chichén Itzá, the Tōnalpōhualli, the *Popol Vuh*, and K'iche' Maya history, mythology and archaeological sites, include:

Popol Vuh: The Sacred Book of the Ancient Quiché Maya. Translated by D. Goetz and S. G. Morley. University of Oklahoma Press, Norman, 1950.

Popol Vuh: *The Mayan Book of the Dawn of Life*. Translated by Dennis Tedlock. A Touchstone Book, Simon & Schuster, 1996.

"Xibalba: Nine-Leveled Underground Place Of Fear Ruled By Lords Of Death In Maya Beliefs," by A. Sutherland, AncientPages.com, May 12, 2020. https://www.ancientpages.com/2020/05/12/xibalba-nine-leveled-underground-place-of-fear-ruled-by-lords-of-death-in-maya-beliefs/

"Xibalba," by Mark Cartwright, *World History Encyclopedia*, October 21, 2004. https://www.worldhistory.org/Xibalba/

"The Conquest of the Maya...a long battle." By Indalecio Cardeña Vázquez. *The Yucatan Times*. January 24, 2020.

"Group of a Thousand Columns in Chichén Itzá," Mayan Peninsula website. https://mayanpeninsula.com/en/thousand-columns-chichen-itza/

"Hunahpú and Xbalanqué — The Maya Hero Twins: The Mayan Myth of the Hero Twins — Stories from the Popol Vuh" by Nicoletta Maestri, ThoughtCo., December 1, 2020. https://www.thoughtco.com/hunahpu-xbalanque-maya-hero-twins-171590

"Who's Who in the *Popol Vuh*," The Bower's Blog, Bower's Museum, posted May 12, 2016. https://www.bowers.org/index.php/collection/collection-blog/who-s-who-in-the-popolvuh#:~:text=Xpiyacoc%20and%20Xmucane%20referred%20to,help%20wooden%20men%20are%20created.

"The Chac Mool Sculptures of Ancient Mexico: Reclining Statues Associated with Mesoamerican Cultures," by Christopher Minster, ThoughtCo., January 26, 2019. https://www.thoughtco.com/chac-mool-sculptures-of-ancient-mexico-2136309

"Creation Story of the Maya," Smithsonian National Museum of the American Indian, Smithsonian Latino Center. https://maya.nmai.si.edu/the-maya/creation-story-maya

"The *Popol Vuh*: The Maya Story of Creation," YouTube, uploaded by Ancient Americas, January 31, 2021. https://www.youtube.com/watch?v=k-tIL-uc2Kuw

"Unearthed: Mayan City of Blood (S1, E1) | Full Episode," YouTube, uploaded by Science Channel, September 16, 2020. https://www.youtube.com/watch?v=oOerY0UPYOk

"Tōnalpōhualli The Human Relationship with Time & Space," with Dr. Alex Mazatl Ojeda YouTube, uploaded by Ehecatl Wind Philosophies, September 16, 2021. https://www.youtube.com/watch?v=Mr_yNNxqgUE

"*Popol Vuh*: The Creation Myth of the Maya (1989) by Patricia Amlin," YouTube, uploaded by Bat Guano, August 12, 2019. https://www.youtube.com/watch?v=FHSOGryN-DA.

"Great Myths and Legends: Hero Twins of the Americas: Myths of Origin, Duality, and Vengeance," YouTube, uploaded by Penn Museum, March 2, 2016. https://www.youtube.com/watch?v=mG-Hi57V2_0

"Lecture 19: Ancient Maya gods, part 1: major deities and narratives," YouTube, uploaded by Alexandre Tokovinine, October 27, 2021. https://www.youtube.com/watch?v=_T1hYTS5vO8

The Xibalbá poems sequence seeks to honor the ancient K'iche' Maya creation text, the *Popol Vuh,* where Xibalbá is mentioned, and highlighted, through imaginative means the fierce importance and impact of this text to decedents of ancient Mesoamerica. Some of the poems in this series focus on the moments in the *Popol Vuh*, where the Hero Twins, Hunahpú and Xbalanqué, go down into the underworld to face the Lords of Xibalbá, including the two primary gods, One Death and Seven Death. In researching, I read how many Mexicans, Mexican Americans, and Latin Americans who learn about the *Popol Vuh* wish the creation text was more imbued in everyday knowledge. These poems become wormholes of the past and present, to extend conversations around the Maya beliefs, Xibalbá, spark curiosity, and engage in imaginative memorying to resist colonization's shadow of erasure.

"Xibalba (n)" contains the following quotes:

> "Our mind has a borderline with the universe, there, where we promenade, and where tragedy resides." Etel Adnan, *Night*, pg. 13. Nightboat Books, 2016.
>
> "It's good to stay in discontinuity, there/ where birds live, [...]/ we manage to bear the unbearable." Etel Adnan, *Time*, page 22, translated by Sarah Riggs. Nightboat Books, 2019.
>
> "Something can be revealed in these moments of distraction." Sara Ahmed, "On Being Directed," *Living a Feminist Life*, pg. 45. Duke University Press, 2017.

"Ecogodliness [I pause at the underbelly of a lily pad]"uses the quote, "When we enter into that closeness and unboundedness, it feels like disintegration, like everywhere," Mei-Mei Berssenbrugge, *A Treatise On Stars*, pg. 67. New Directions Publishing, 2020.

"Earthly Rhythms" contains the quote "high cultural tolerance for women's suffering" is from Rebecca Thurston, professor of psychiatry at the University of Pittsburgh in the article by Susan Dominus, "The Sunday Read: 'Women Have Been Mislead About Menopause'," February 12, 2023. https://www.nytimes.com/2023/02/12/podcasts/the-daily/menopause-treatment-hormone-therapy.html.

The photos in "Xibalbá :: Creation" and "Hunger Sonnet" are from my trip to Chichén Itzá in Summer 2022. It rained the entire time. I felt this sign.

In "Hint: An Ars Poetica Triptych on Relationship" the third section, the phrase "Keeper of ribs, an understudy of bone" is in conversation with Oliver Baez Bendorf's poem, "Bone Dust" in *Consider the Rooster*, pg. 74-77. Nightboat Books, 2024.

In "Remembering Etel Adnan While Filling Out the Ohio Power of Attorney Before the Mastectomy," the italic texts are direct quotes from Etel Adnan, *Night*, pg. 35. Nightboat Books, 2016.

In the poem "Plaything," the title "Mexico Asks Vatican for Temporary Return of Ancient Indigenous Manuscripts," along with the words ""difficult anniversaries" and the quote from Mexican President Andrés Manuel López Obrado, "the arrival of the Spanish 500 years ago to present-day Mexican lands cannot be judged in light of contemporary considerations," are all from the article, "Mexico Asks Vatican for Temporary Return of Ancient Indigenous Manuscripts," Valentia Di Liscia, *Hyperallergic* online, October, October 29, 2020; https://hyperallergic.com/598115/mexico-asks-vatican-for-temporary-return-of-ancient-indigenous-manuscripts/. The two images of Codex Borgia, Loubat 1898, #2 and #71, Courtesy of Ancient Americas at LACMA (ancientamericas.org)

The bottom photo in "Enoughness (n) (v)" was taken on the day of my last chemotherapy session, after five months of treatment. The top photo was taken on the day of my last radiation session, after 25 sessions of treatment spanning five weeks. I was unaware of the tradition of bell ringing after each stage of cancer treatment completion. Each time the nurses asked me to read the plaque on the wall, I cried. Thinking of the words "Ring this bell three times well..." makes me choke up.

"we have to learn to turn toward," Sara Ahmed, "Feminism Is Sensational," *Living a Feminist Life*, pg. 32. Duke University Press, 2017.

"Xibalbá :: Holes," mentions Garza and the quote, "sometimes a rectangle is a sacred shape," Cristina Rivera Garza, *The Taiga Syndrome*, pg. 69. Translated by Suzanne Jill Levine & Aviva Kana. Dorothy, A Publishing Project, 2018.

"Inner" contains the quote, ""Our psyches resemble the bordertowns [...] Nothing happens in the "real" world unless it first happens in the images in our heads." Gloria Anzaldúa, "Towards a New Consciousness," *Borderlands/La Frontera: The New Mestiza*. Aunt Lute Books, 1987.

"On Divination" contains the quote, "I am attempting my own/ myth-making," Solmaz Sharif, "PERSONAL EFFECTS," *Look*, pg 63. Graywolf Press, 2016.

"Xibalbá :: Unmyth" is in conversation with Sandra Ruiz's line "half-life right behind my teeth" in the poem "Fog Play," *Left Turns in Brown Study*, pg. 76. Duke University Press, 2025.

In "Ecogodliness [Christensen wonders where art necessitates, our story of the world]" is in conversation with Inger Christensen's poem, "Our Story About the World," *The Condition of Secrecy: Selected Essays*, translated by Susanna Nied, pg. 24. New Directions, 2018.

In Gratitude

This book was a journey—across the world, across time, and across my own body topography. I honor the ancestors, the deities in the Codex Yoalli Ehēcatl, and the voices of those who empire tries to eradicate. As a descendant of ancient Mesoamerica, in all this research, I fully know that I am not alone. Ollin—the movement of my lineage—reverberates inside me, inside all of us who seek to know our existences before and after colonization. To my Latine beloveds, may we continue to trace ourselves into liberation.

Deepest gratitude to my beloveds whose belief in me and my poetry makes all of this poetical existence possible. Mel and Joe, fighting cancer was less terrifying because of your love. You flew back and forth from CO week-over-week to take care of me, to dole out medication, to sleep with the dogs, to check on me every twenty minutes after chemo, to just *be* beside me. Chris, you held my hand, patiently gave me space while I cried, made me laugh every day, stroked my peach fuzz saying, "You can almost run your fingers through it," and relentlessly told me you loved me. Chris, Mel, Joe...without you I would not be able to fathom recovery and a future of recovery. The ripples of beloveds—Beth, Bruce, Mindy, Shi, Diana, TC, Foula, Kay, Stephanie, S.A., Cathy, Mom, Lauren, Jack, Tammy, Mark, Wes, Jenn, Renee, Paul, Isaac, Escher, Jess, Heather, John, SueEllen, Ausma, Katie Y., Sharrell, Leah, Jenny, Katie B., and Joanna—your support was felt in unimaginable ways.

These poems dwell in ancestry and community that bolstered my mind and body at the most frightening and tender moments of my life. Cancer is in these pages—yet this is not a book on cancer, it's a book on *homecoming* amidst the trials of living.

Infinite hugs to my current and former students who wander and wonder with me on the importance of poetry in our lives, our poetic existences.

I am immensely grateful to Noemi Press—Suzi F. Garcia, Anthony Cody, Sarah Gzemzki, Mariah Bosch, Roda Avelar, Auden Eagerton, and the entire press team—thank you for seeing the importance of this book. Massive mil gracias to my editors, Suzi and Mariah for making all this magic happen. Another huge thank-you to Roda Avelar for her design expertise, attention, and labor creating the front and back covers, as well as the interior design. Thank you to Mai Der Vang, Erika L. Sánchez, and Douglas Kearney for their generous words and spending time in these pages. While writing, I received support from the Charles Phelps Taft Research Center at the University of Cincinnati including a 2023 Charles P. Taft Faculty Summer Research Fellowship, an Ohio Arts Council Individual Excellence Award, and a Tin House Next Book Writer's Residency.

Thank you to Dr. Claudia Montuschi, Scriptor Latinus, Director of the Manuscripts Department at the Vatican Apostolic Library, for communicating and arranging my visit to study the Codex Yoalli Ehēcatl.

Thank you to the Los Angeles County Museum of Art (LACMA) Ancient American's Department for the use of the high-resolution images of the Codex

Yoalli Ehēcatl (Borgia) and drawings by Linda Schele, David Schele, and Mark van Stone.

Appreciation to the editors and publishing teams of the following literary journals, magazines, and anthologies in which these poems first found literary homes. Many of these poems were in different formats when first published.

32 Poems, "Ecogodliness [A large solar flare]"
Academy of American Poets *Poem-a-Day*, "Inner"
AGNI, Portfolio of Central American and Mexican Diaspora Writing, "Undulations :: Plate 73," "Undulations :: Plate 53," "Undulations :: Plate 44," "Undulations :: Plate 39," and "Undulations :: Plate 8"
Alaska Quarterly Review, "Xibalbá :: Consume" and "Earthly Rhythms"
The American Poetry Review, "Undulations :: Plate 22," "Undulations :: Plate 26," "Undulations :: Plate 29" and "Xibalbá :: Offerings"
Barrelhouse Review, Latine Monster's Edition, "Xibalbá :: Unbearable" (previously titled "I am La Llorona in the Exam Room at the Breast Cancer Center")
Brevity, "Xibalbá :: Ritual"
Copper Nickel, "Xibalbá :: Wilt"
Dark Mountain, "Ecogodliness [Scrolling the news]"
Gulf Coast, ""Xibalbá" and "Xibalbá :: Baby Teeth"
The Iowa Review, "Upon Remembering the Statistic" and "Science of Undoing"
The Kenyon Review, "Summoning Huixtocihuatl at My Annual Physical" and "Ecogodliness [Christensen wonders where art...]"
The Missouri Review, "Ecogodliness," Poem of the Week Feature.
The Nation, "17 Days After Mastectomy & Axillary Dissection of Lymph Nodes: A Love Poem"
Notre Dame Review. "Archive Notes #4" and "Archive Notes #5"
Poetry Magazine, "Xibalbá :: Tunneling," "I Carry a Wor{l}ld Inside Me," and "Xibalbá :: Ritual"
Ploughshares, "Xibalbá :: Holes"
Prairie Schooner, "Archive Notes #1"
Virginia Quarterly Review, *"Message to the Skeletal Earth Goddess," "Message to the Young Goddess of the Moon," "Message to the Goddess of Running Water," "Message to Rabbit in the Moon," and "Xibalbá :: Shape"*
Water & Stone Review, "Ecogodliness [You trace the sundogs]" and "Always Incomplete," (now "On Unknowing")
Zócalo Public Square, "Etiology of Wound in the Wound" (now "Hunger Sonnet")

A version of the poem "On Blessings & Want" is in Air, Vol. 2, *Elementals*, an anthology dedicated to the four elements of Earth, air, fire and water. Gavin Van Horn & Bruce Jennings, series editors. Nickole Brown & Craig Santos Perez, poetry editors. Published by the Center for Humans & Nature Press in the U.S., the publishing wing of the Center for Humans & Nature.

"Ecogodliness," appears in *The Ecopoetry Anthology: Volume II*, Trinity University Press.

The poems, "Xibalba :: Creation," and "Xibalba :: Consume," are a part of the anthology, *IXPAHTLI: New Chicane Prose*, University of New Mexico Press, edited by ire'ne lara silva.

Felicia Zamora is the author of seven books of poetry including *Interstitial Archaeology*, Wisconsin Poetry Series (2025), *Quotient* (2022), *I Always Carry My Bones*, winner of the 2020 Iowa Poetry Prize (2021) and the 2022 Ohioana Book Award in Poetry, *Body of Render*, Benjamin Saltman Award winner (2020), and *Of Form & Gather*, Andrés Montoya Poetry Prize winner (2017). She's won the Loraine Williams Poetry Prize, C.P. Cavafy Prize, Wabash Prize, Tomaž Šalamun Prize, and two Ohio Arts Council Individual Excellence Awards (2024 & 2022). She has been supported by a Tin House Next Book Residency, Yaddo Residency, Ragdale Fellowship, and CantoMundo Fellowship. Her writing appears in Academy of American Poets *Poem-A-Day, AGNI, Alaska Quarterly Review, American Poetry Review, Best American Poetry 2022, Boston Review, Brevity, Ecotone, The Georgia Review, Guernica, Gulf Coast, Indiana Review, Iowa Review, Kenyon Review, Lit Hub, Missouri Review, Orion, Ploughshares, Poetry Magazine, The Nation, West Branch*, and others. She is a professor of poetry and a 2025-2026 Taft Research Center Fellow at the University of Cincinnati, a poetry editor for *Colorado Review*, and a contributing editor for *West Branch*.